# Lancashire's Easiest Walks

## Doug and Margaret Ratcliffe

**Published by** Sigma Leisure – an imprint of
Sigma Press, Stobart House, Pontyclerc, Penybanc Road
Ammanford, Carmarthenshire SA18 3HP

**British Library Cataloguing in Publication Data**

A CIP record for this book is available from the British Library

**ISBN:** 978-1-85058-892-4

**Typesetting and Design by:** Sigma Press, Ammanford, Carms

**Maps:** Doug Ratcliffe

**Photographs:** Doug and Margaret Ratcliffe

**Cover:** The windmill on Lytham Green

**Printed by:** Berforts Group Ltd, Stevenage

**Disclaimer:** The information in this book is given in good faith and is believed to be correct at the time of publication. No responsibility is accepted by either the author or publisher for errors or omissions, or for any loss or injury howsoever caused. Only you can judge your own fitness, competence and experience.

# Preface

Lancashire has a lot to offer the disabled visitor. The low-lying coastline has mile after mile of promenades and level surfaced paths, which are well served with disabled toilets. In addition there are several country parks throughout the county that have been upgraded for disabled use in recent years, including at least two which offer pre-booked mobility scooters for hire free of charge.

Some of the paths described in this book are steeper and have rougher surfaces than others, but they should all be accessible for pushchairs and, at least, partially accessible for manual wheelchair users. It can't be stressed too strongly that the suitability of any path for people with limited mobility depends not only on the type of wheelchair being used (manual, powered, or mobility scooter), but also on the physical fitness of both the wheelchair user and of his or her carer. If you find you're having difficulty on any of the walks, turn back straight away. I've completed all of these walks using a standard powered wheelchair without difficulty, but know for a fact that I would need to turn back in a few places if I was using my lightweight mobility scooter and I might need to turn back in my manual wheelchair, depending on who was pushing me. Potentially difficult sections are mentioned under 'Path Quality' for each walk.

Although essentially a book for wheelchair users, the paths are equally suitable for young children and toddlers in pushchairs. With this in mind the location of children's playgrounds have been noted and marked on the maps.

Many entries also have a 'Points Of Interest' section describing features that can be seen from the paths, and the photographs included illustrate the fact that a wheelchair or pushchair is no barrier to the Lancashire's varied scenery. We hope that you enjoy the walks as much as we have.

Doug and Margaret Ratcliffe
September 2011

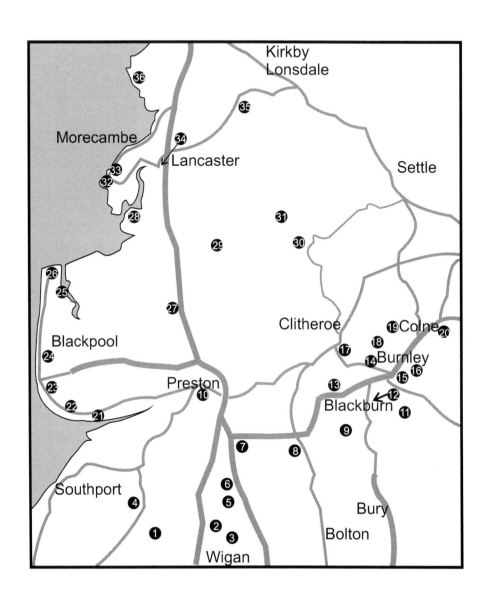

Kirkby
Lonsdale

36

35

Morecambe
34

Lancaster

Settle

33
32

28

31

29

30

26

25

27

Clitheroe

19 Colne
20

Blackpool

18

17

Burnley
14

16

24

15

23

13

12

Preston

Blackburn
11

10

9

22

21

Southport

7

8

4

6

5

Bury

2

Bolton

1

3

Wigan

# Contents

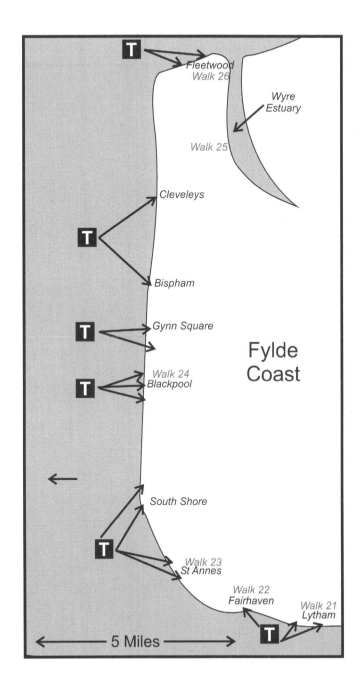

T — Fleetwood
Walk 26

Wyre
Estuary

Walk 25

Cleveleys

T

Bispham

Gynn Square

T

Fylde
Coast

Walk 24
Blackpool

T

South Shore

T

Walk 23
St Annes

Walk 22
Fairhaven

Walk 21
Lytham

T

← 5 Miles →

# An Overview of The Fylde Coast

The Fylde Coast provides a unique opportunity for an extended wheelchair coastal route on mainly level tarmac for an amazing 18 miles. There is one 1¼ mile stretch between St Annes and Blackpool South Shore where sand dunes block a view of the sea, and it is necessary to skirt them on a pavement besides the busy A584. Apart from this the route consists of a succession of promenades and paths alongside the sea defences or on the sandy heaths and low cliffs that link the main towns.

There are several disabled toilets along the route placed at fairly regular intervals, as shown on the map on page 6. Several of them are a new design which can be opened for free with a RADAR key, or for parents needing the baby changing facility they are also coin-operated (20p). There are car parks with disabled spaces and roadside parking places too numerous to mention along the whole route. Car parking details are included for the five walks chosen. If you are a blue badge holder it is advisable to check on parking charges. At some car parks on the Fylde coast you can only park for free if you use a disabled space. If you use an ordinary parking space you have to pay, but this rule doesn't apply everywhere.

I have chosen five separate shorter walks on the Fylde coast. Between them, they include most of the highlights and points of interest, illustrating the contrast between relatively lonely sandy heaths and crowded brash seaside resorts that exist along the route. These are:

|  |  |
|---|---|
| Walk 21 | Lytham, Promenade |
| Walk 22 | Lytham, Fairhaven Lake |
| Walk 23 | St Anne's, Promenade |
| Walk 24 | Blackpool Tower |
| Walk 26 | Fleetwood, Promenade |

## *Key to Maps*

*The sketch maps are not accurate and are intended simply to give an overview of the walks.   They should  be used in conjunction with the relevant Ordnance Survey Map.*

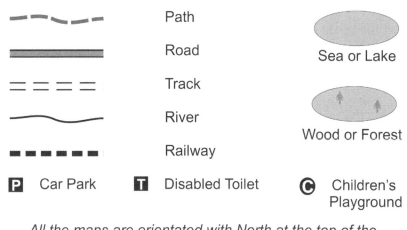

Path

Road

Sea or Lake

Track

River

Wood or Forest

Railway

**P** Car Park        **T** Disabled Toilet        **C** Children's Playground

*All the maps are orientated with North at the top of the page and all are drawn to different scales, as indicated on each map.*

# 1. Beacon Country Park, Up Holland

This 300 acre hillside park has spectacular views over the extraordinarily flat expanse of the Lancashire plain. It consists of a mixture of mature woodland and wide open rolling grassland and includes a nature trail, picnic sites and a children's playground.'

| | |
|---|---|
| **Distance** | Circular walk of about ¾ of a mile |
| **Path quality** | Smooth paths of compacted pebbles/earth with mainly gentle gradients |
| **Car Parking** | From the M58 Junction 5 take the A577 towards Wigan and follow the brown tourist signs 'Beacon Country Park. When you arrive at the park go along Mill Lane, past the first two car parks and take the next left signposted 'Beacon Golf Course and Country Park'. The car park is just down this lane and is shared by the golf club and the country park. There are five disabled parking spaces. There are also a further five disabled parking spaces at the Carr Lane car park (the second car park you have already passed) but it doesn't have any other facilities |
| **Disabled toilet** | On the main car park. There are also a disabled toilet for customers in the golf clubhouse if you decide to eat there |
| **Grid reference** | SD505066 |
| **Map** | OS Explorer Map OL21 |

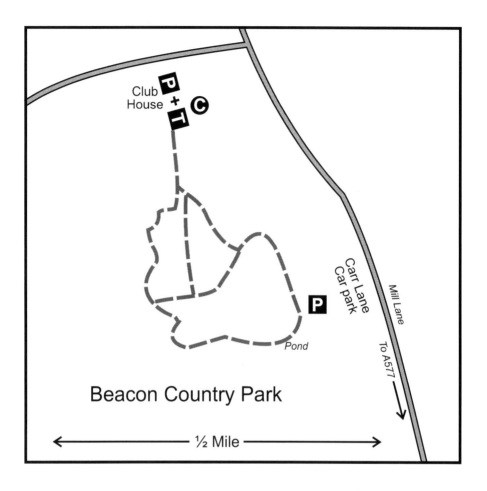

Beacon Country Park

## Directions

The path starts from the far end of the car park. Go over the wooden bridge then turn down to the right through the woods. The path climbs out into open meadowland with spectacular views over the flat Lancashire plain towards the coast.

Continuing on, the path passes a small pond with a wheelchair accessible boardwalk across the marshy area that borders it. At the disabled car park at Carr Lane car park, a path is signposted back through the trees to the Visitor Centre.

## Points of Interest

The park gets its name from Ashurst Beacon, a stone spire on top of the hill behind the park that marks the spot where signals used to be sent across the country from one hilltop to the next.

At the Countryside Ranger's office, next to the small Visitor Centre on the car park, all-terrain mobility scooters, called trampers, can be borrowed free of charge. These enable you to explore virtually anywhere in the park, except for those paths which have steps of course. A map showing the recommended route for trampers is also available. It is necessary to book trampers in advance and to have a short induction session before you use them for the first time (see further details on this in 'Points of Interest' for Walk 29).

*The boardwalk across the marsh*

# 2. Worthington Lakes, Standish

A very pleasant short walk around these lakes accompanied by resident flocks of geese and ducks. The circular walk around the smaller lake is virtually level throughout and is particularly suitable for manual wheelchair users.

| | |
|---|---|
| **Distance** | ¾ mile circular walk round the smaller lake. The linear path from the car park to the concrete drain at the far corner of the larger lake (point A) is 1½ miles return |
| **Path quality** | Good quality compacted gravel and mainly level with some short inclines at the side of the larger lake |
| **Car Parking** | About 5 miles South of Chorley on the A5106. Worthington Lakes is signposted to the left just after the 'Lakeside Care Home'. There are 2 disabled parking spaces on the upper car park |
| **Disabled toilet** | Near the disabled parking spaces. A RADAR key is required |
| **Grid reference** | SD580106 |
| **Map** | OS Explorer Map 285 |

## Directions

From the car park go down past the education centre and turn left along the lakeside. At the end of the first lake you can either turn right between the lakes, to complete a circuit of the smaller lake, or continue on alongside the larger lake, as far as point A where a deep concrete open drain restricts access for wheelchairs. I did manage to get across this obstacle, with considerable help, in a standard powered wheelchair but later regretted doing so because, on the far bank of the lake, there is a section where the path is very narrow with a four foot drop at one side straight into the water. This is definitely not recommended!

## Points of Interest

Worthington Lakes consist of three reservoirs which were built in the nineteenth century to serve the rapidly increasing industrial areas

*The path alongside the smaller lake*

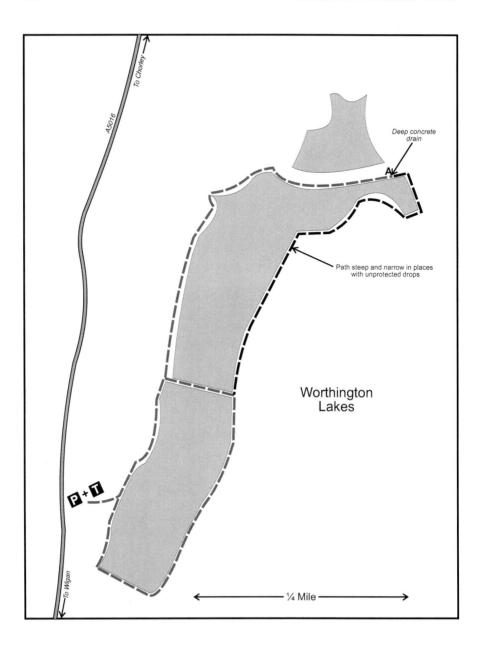

To Chorley

A5016

Deep concrete
drain

A

Path steep and narrow in places
with unprotected drops

Worthington
Lakes

P + T

To Wigan

¼ Mile

around Wigan. They are fed by the River Douglas which rises in the Pennine moors and continues on to enter the Ribble Estuary downstream from Preston.

Today the Lakes form part of a 50 acre country park with accessible footpaths, a tapping rail for the visually impaired, and an education centre for field studies by local school children.

*Being greeted by the local residents*

# 3. Haigh Hall, Wigan

The 250 acre Haigh Hall Country Park is a delight for wheelchair users with a large network of generally well surfaced paths with gentle gradients. The mature woodland contains an impressive variety of trees and bushes and it is interspersed with open areas of grassland. The whole park is well planned and well managed.

| | |
|---|---|
| **Distance** | Circular walk past the children's playground, round the walled garden then right at point A to join the main drive and back past the Hall is 1½ miles in length. The linear walk down the main drive to the old railway cutting is 3 miles return |
| **Path quality** | The main drive is tarmac and the path through the wood past the walled garden is fairly smooth compacted gravel. Gradients on the recommended routes are gentle. There are many other paths in the country park to explore, some of which are rougher and with steeper gradients than others |
| **Car Parking** | From M61 Junction 6 take signs for (A6) and then follow the brown tourist signs 'Haigh Hall Country Park'. After about 3 miles turn left in front of the Balcarres Arms, down Copperas Lane, and the car park is about ½ mile down on the left behind the Stables Café and Information Centre |
| **Disabled toilet** | On the outside of the Stables Centre facing the Hall |
| **Grid reference** | SD601088 |
| **Map** | OS Explorer Map 285 |

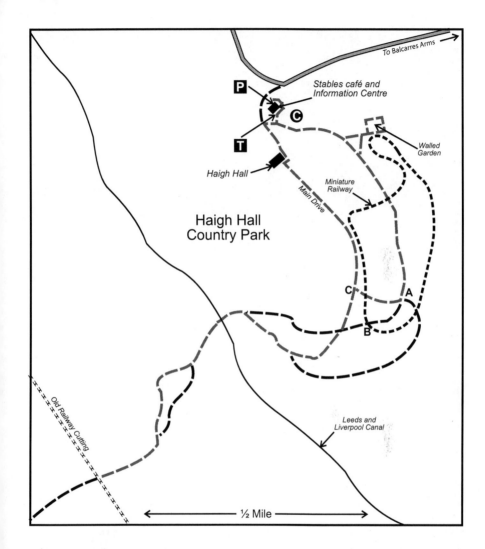

## Directions

From the car park go round in front of the Stables Café and Information Centre and continue on to your left past the children's playground, which is suitable for children of all ages. Continuing on the main path, the walled garden on your left is a haven of peace and tranquillity and is well worth a short detour.

*Inside the walled garden*

At the crossroads at point A it is advisable to turn right. If you go straight on the level crossing at point B is difficult in a wheelchair, and the path to the left is quite steep and bumpy in places. At point C you can either turn right to return to the car park, up the main drive and past the Hall, or turn left to explore further down the main drive. You pass over a delightful Canal Bridge and continue on through the trees to a bridge over the deep cutting of a disused railway. The drive continues on but it is probably advisable to return at this point as the route becomes increasingly steep.

## Points of Interest

There has been a Hall at Haigh since the 12th century but the present building dates from 1840. It was built by James Lindsay, Earl of Crawford and Balcarres, but was sold to Wigan Corporation in 1947. The Lindsay family had lived at Haigh since 1780. They developed coal mining and iron founding on the estate and the Isle of Man's Laxey Wheel was reputedly made here. The delightful grounds we see today were laid out in the 1860s to hide these industrial workings and to provide employment for local cotton workers, who were suffering during the cotton famine caused by the American Civil War. Haigh Hall is currently used as a corporate conference centre and as a venue for weddings.

# 4. Mere Sands Wood, Rufford

A pleasant woodland walk on level good quality paths, with bird-watching hides along the way looking out over a series of shallow woodland lakes. There is a Visitor Centre with information on the wild life that can be seen.

| | |
|---|---|
| **Distance** | The recommended circular wheelchair walk is 1¼ miles plus short detours for the hides. The total length of paths accessible for most wheelchairs is about 3 miles |
| **Path quality** | Very smooth compacted pebbles and gravel, some short mild slopes but virtually level throughout |
| **Car Parking** | Turn left off the A59 Liverpool to Preston road at Rufford on the B5246. About 1 mile down this road turn left at a low wooden sign 'Mere Sands Wood Nature Reserve'. The car park is at the end of this lane |
| **Disabled toilet** | Inside the Visitor Centre |
| **Grid reference** | SD447159 |
| **Map** | OS Explorer Map 285 |

## Directions
There is a map on an information board near the car park and it is also printed on a leaflet available from the Visitor Centre. Basically, it's just a circular route round the outside of the woods with a link path across the centre. Everything is well signposted on the way round.

## Points of Interest

Mere Sands Wood is owned by The Wildlife Trust and is a Site of Special Scientific Interest. The area is important because it consists of alternate layers of sand and peat, which were laid down in the last ice age over the underlying boulder clay of the Lancashire plain, and it has remained largely undisturbed since that time. These unique geological features have enabled The Wildlife Trust to encourage many more species of animals and plants to become established here.

The lakes were formed by the extraction of sand which was found to be suitable for the glass making industry. Extraction of sand occurred between 1974 and 1982 and planning restrictions ensured that the perimeter trees of the woods, a screen for the workings, were undisturbed. This also helped preserve some of the wildlife in the woods and gave The Wildlife Trust a head start when they took over the site in 1982. Since then much work has been done to improve the site for both wildlife and visitors, and development is ongoing today.

*View from one of the hides*

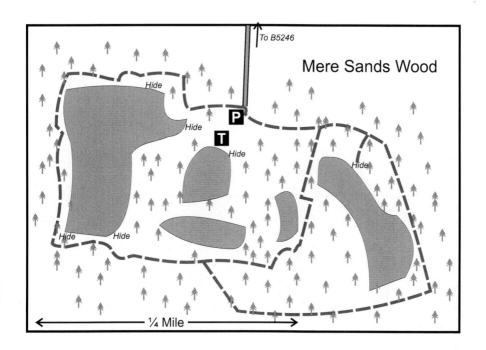

To B5246

Mere Sands Wood

¼ Mile

# 5. Yarrow Valley Country Park, Chorley

This is a delightful lakeside, riverside and woodland walk which abounds with wildlife. It is difficult to believe that the whole 700-acre site was formerly heavily industrialised and the country park thoroughly deserves its Green Flag status.

| | |
|---|---|
| **Distance** | 1½ miles circular walk round the reservoir and the big lodge and a further mile there and back to see the fish ladder |
| **Path quality** | Good quality crushed stone surface and mainly level except for a short initial slope up from the car park |
| **Car Parking** | Yarrow Valley Country Park is signposted to the right off the B5251 Coppull to Chorley road, about ½ mile from Coppull. The car park is at the end of Birkacre Road. There are 3 disabled parking spaces |
| **Disabled toilet** | On the side of the Visitor Centre. The toilets are open daily during Visitor Centre hours |
| **Grid reference** | SD571152 |
| **Map** | OS Explorer Map 285 |

## Directions
Take the sloping path up from the car park to the right of the Visitor Centre, turning left near the top to follow the path round the small reservoir, then bear left again to continue on round the big lodge. At the far end of the big lodge (point A), the path to the left leads on to

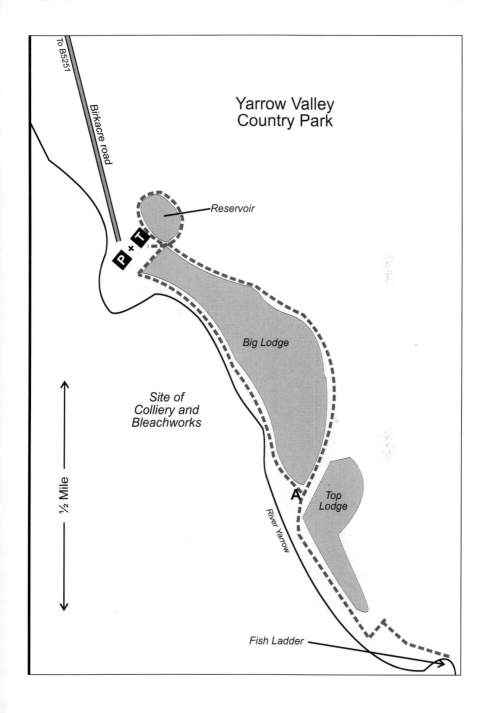

a waterfall with an impressive fish ladder constructed on the far bank of the river, whilst the path to the right completes the circuit of the big lodge.

## Points of Interest

The car park is the site of Chorley's first powered cotton spinning mill, built by Sir Richard Arkwright to house his new spinning frame, which replaced the Spinning Jenny invented by James Hargreaves. The mill put Chorley on the map as one of the most important towns of the industrial revolution but it was burned down in 1779 by rioters opposed to mechanisation in the mills.

The Visitor Centre has information on the natural history of the site and a full programme of events are organised for both adults and children throughout the year. Note that the water level in the top lodge

*The fish ladder*

has been lowered deliberately to create a wetland habitat for wildlife. When the weir was built to divert water from the river Yarrow into the mill lodges, it had the unfortunate effect of preventing fish from proceeding up the river, to the feeder streams in the Pennine foothills, to spawn. Since the building of the fish ladder, however, large numbers of trout can now be seen travelling upstream, usually during October, and salmon have also been seen in the river.

# 6. Astley Park, Chorley

A delightful free visit to a magnificent building with a most colourful and interesting history, surrounded by very pleasant parkland with a choice of routes available.

| | |
|---|---|
| **Distance** | There are about 2 miles of wheelchair accessible paths |
| **Path quality** | Most paths are fairly level and tarmaced except for the woodland walk, which is compacted earth/gravel and is fairly smooth. The path leading from the Hall down towards the Southport Road entrance is steep in places and there is a short section of path at point B with 2 or 3 individual steps that are impassable for most wheelchairs |
| **Car Parking** | From the M61 Junction 8 go towards Chorley and turn left at the first roundabout, right at the second and left at the third (signposted 'Astley Hall' on a brown tourist sign). Go down this road for about ¾ mile and Astley Hall is signposted down a road on the left. Park in the car park at the end of the road |
| **Disabled toilet** | In the Coach House, next to the Hall |
| **Grid reference** | SD574184 |
| **Map** | OS Explorer Map 285 |

## Directions

From the car park follow the signpost down a short link path to Astley Park. The Hall is to your left just past the Coach House. As the map shows there are several routes to explore. If you can manage hills, the

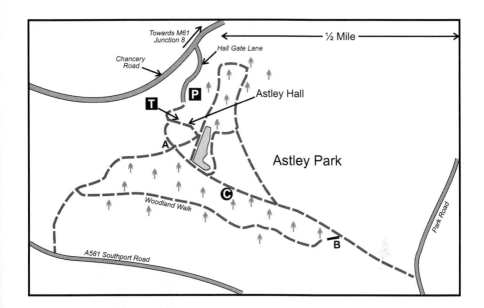

woodland walk makes a nice contrast from the predominantly open grassland of the rest of the park. Take the path signposted 'Tennis Bowls Putting' from point A in front of the Hall. Go down the Hill and just after the bridge over the stream, take an unsurfaced path off to the right. This path follows the edge of the park through delightful woodland to point B, where a short inaccessible section means it's necessary to return by the same route.

## Points of Interest
Only the ground floor of Astley Hall is accessible for wheelchairs but there are several rooms well worth exploring. Don't miss the incredible plasterwork on the ceiling of the entrance hall.

Astley Hall's magnificent and unique architecture is a result of upgrades over the years designed to demonstrate the owner's wealth and prestige. It is included in Simon Jenkins book *Britain's Best 1000 houses* and is certainly one of the most important architecturally historic houses in Lancashire.

The Hall has had something of a colourful history. It was rebuilt in Elizabethan times by the Charnock family who were Catholics and supporters of the monarchy in the English civil war. John Charnock was executed for high treason in 1586 for supporting Mary Queen of Scots in her attempt to dethrone Queen Elizabeth. The family was also fined heavily by parliament for its support of King Charles. They ran grave risks as practicing Catholics during this time and, in 2004, during restoration work on the chimneys, a long forgotten priest hole was discovered near the fireplace in one of the bedrooms.

In the eighteenth century Astley Hall was inherited through marriage by the Towneley-Parker family of Cuerden Hall (Walk 7), and in 1922 it was obtained by Chorley Corporation and opened to the public.

*Astley Hall*

# 7. Cuerden Valley Park, Bamber Bridge

A pleasant walk on tarmac paths in the former grounds and the gardens of Cuerden Hall. The path alongside the river is essentially level but paths up to the Hall and Visitor Centre, over the bridges at point A and point B, are fairly steep. Unfortunately in parts of the park, at busy times, there is constant background traffic noise from the nearby motorway.

## Directions

The path into Cuerden Valley Park starts from Sheep Hill car park and carries on along the river valley for about ¾ mile, where it forks at point B. If you take the left fork it leads to a bridge over the river and then sweeps uphill towards Cuerden Hall. A path goes off to the right, but continue straight on through a car park to join Berkeley Drive. Turn left and the Visitor Centre is a little way down on the right.

To explore the Hall's gardens, turn left out of the Visitor Centre back along Berkeley Drive and, after a few yards, take a path on the left signposted 'coffee and gift shop' and follow it round to Cuerden Hall.

*Cuerden Hall*

| Distance | About 2½ miles there and back including the various paths in the Hall's gardens and pinetum |
|---|---|
| Path quality | Tarmac surface throughout. The path is mainly level from the car park up to point A or point B, but rises fairly steeply up to Cuerden Hall and the Visitor Centre |
| Car Parking | Turn right off the A6 Preston to Chorley road onto the B5256, at the third roundabout, after crossing the M6 at Junction 29. Go straight across the next roundabout and Sheep Hill car park is on the right at the bottom of the hill. Alternatively there are 3 disabled parking spaces in front of the Visitor Centre. Take the next right after Sheep Hill Car Park down Shady Lane and then after about ½ mile turn right down Berkeley Drive |
| Disabled toilet | At the Visitor Centre during opening hours (Monday to Friday 9am to 5pm). At other times the nearest disabled toilet is at Bamber Bridge behind the Somerfield supermarket on Station Road. Retrace your journey back along the A6, turning right shortly after crossing the M6 onto the B6258. The Somerfield supermarket is about ¾ mile on the right |
| Grid reference | SD568229 |
| Map | OS Explorer Map 286 |

Go down the side of the hall turning left at the bottom to join the original track at point C. Turn right here and take the second kissing gate on the left (opposite the large sun dial) to explore the American garden and pinetum. If you take the first kissing gate, however, it leads you down to a bridge over the river at point A, and hence along the valley path back to the car park.

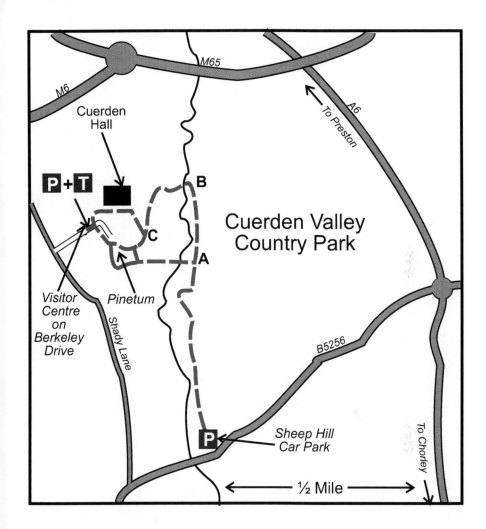

## Points of Interest

The 600 acre Cureden Country Park is based on the parkland belonging originally to the imposing Cuerden Hall, which is now a Sue Ryder Home. The Hall was rebuilt in 1816 and the design of its impressive gardens also date from that time. Features retained from this Victorian heritage include a fine American garden and pinetum, a walled orchard and a small lake.

# 8. Sunnyhurst Wood, Darwen

Sunnyhurst Wood is an oasis of green in an urban landscape. As you walk up the delightful small valley you feel as though you are miles away from the houses and streets that actually surround it.

| Distance | 1¼ miles in total there and back |
|---|---|
| **Path quality** | Good quality fairly level gravel paths throughout |
| **Car Parking** | Take the A666 Blackburn to Darwen road and Sunnyhurst Wood is signposted to the right (brown tourist sign) about half a mile past the turning for the M65 Junction 4. As you drive up Earnsdale Road park on the road near the blue sign 'Disabled Entrance, Sunnyhurst Wood, No cars Allowed' if you do not have blue disabled parking badge. Blue badge holders should ignore this entrance and continue on to the brown sign 'Sunnyhurst Wood, Visitors Centre, Olde England Kiosk'. Drive down this road ignoring the 'No Entry' signs and park at the bottom of the hill near the Drinking Fountain Monument |
| **Disabled toilet** | Past the Visitor Centre just before the Olde England Kiosk on the right. A RADAR key is required |
| **Grid reference** | SD679230 |
| **Map** | OS Explorer Map 287 |

## Directions
From the Drinking Fountain Monument take the main path in either direction, ignoring the various side access paths that lead uphill out

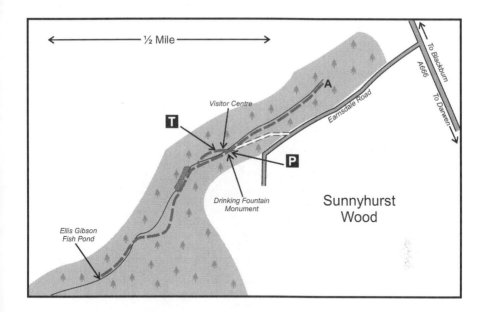

of the valley. An exception to this, however, is the short loop path over the bridge past the Visitor Centre and the toilets.

If you go upstream, past the paddling pool, it is advisable not to go past the Ellis Gibson Fish Pond because the track becomes increasingly steep and rough beyond here. Similarly, if you take the path downstream, it is advisable to return at point A where the path forks.

## Points of Interest

The area around Sunnyhurst Wood was originally open farmland which was planted with trees, in the nineteenth century, to provide cover for game birds. The valley was bought by Darwen Corporation in 1902, to commemorate the coronation of Edward VII, 'for the use of the people of Darwen for all time'.

The Visitors Centre is situated in the Old Keepers Cottage. It is not wheelchair accessible but does have a lovely cottage garden to the front. In the Visitor Centre there is information on various aspects of the woods and children's activities are also available.

The Olde England Kiosk is a Tudor style building, built as a tea rooms in 1912 to commemorate the coronation of King George V.

There are several interesting commemorative bridges over Sunnyhurst Brook, such as the one shown below, which was built by a local wallpaper manufacturer in 1912.

*The Huntington Bridge*

# 9. Calf Hey Reservoir, Haslingden

A circular walk round a reservoir high up on the West Pennine Moors with long distance views down the Rossendale Valley. A semicircular kissing gate at the start of this walk is accessible for most wheelchairs, but unfortunately not for larger mobility scooters.

| | |
|---|---|
| **Distance** | 1¼ miles circular walk |
| **Path quality** | Partly tarmac and partly good quality compacted gravel. There are steep hills down to the dam wall and on the tarmac roadway on the last part of the walk. The path round the far side of the reservoir is level |
| **Car Parking** | Take the A6177 Haslingden to Blackburn road and after about two miles Clough Head Car Park is signposted on the right. There are 2 disabled parking spaces and a disabled toilet here but the walk does not start from this car park. Return back down the A6177 for about ¼ mile and take the first turning on the right. After about 200 yards this road ends at Calf Hey Reservoir car park |
| **Disabled toilet** | At Clough Head car park. A RADAR key is required |
| **Grid reference** | SD754228 |
| **Map** | OS Explorer Map 287 |

## Directions
Go through the kissing gate at the far end of the car park and down the hill, taking the path off to the left at the bottom. Continue down

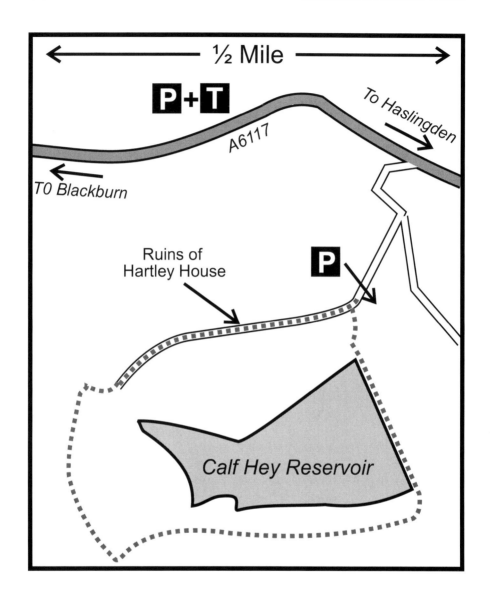

*Calf Hey Reservoir*

to the dam wall and follow the path round the reservoir. At the far end of the reservoir the path joins a tarmac track that leads back to the car park.

## Points of Interest

The valley of Haslingden Grane, where Calf Hey reservoir lies, had the dubious distinction in the nineteenth century as the centre of an illegal whiskey distilling industry.

The walk passes the ruins of Hartley House which dates back to Elizabethan times. The inhabitants were tenant farmers who scratched a living from the land supplemented by hand weaving looms. As you look around at the bleak landscape you can appreciate how hard life must have been high up in this remote valley. Nineteenth century census returns show a gradual decline in the number of families living at this site and it was finally abandoned early in the twentieth century.

# 10. Avenham Park and Riverside, Preston

A delightful municipal park situated partly on a very steep hillside, a pleasant riverside walk and a linear nature reserve along the track of an old railway line. The first time I visited Avenham Park I was amazed to find open countryside so close to the city centre.

| | |
|---|---|
| **Distance** | The circular riverside walk as described below is 3¾ miles. The linear nature reserve walk along the bed of the old railway is up to 4 miles return from the bridge over the River Ribble |
| **Path quality** | Tarmac throughout. Most of the paths are level except for a few important exceptions. The paths from the entrances to Avenham Park on the city side down to the River Ribble are fairly long and they vary from steep to very steep. At point A there are very steep short descents both along the riverside and down to the bridge. I needed help to negotiate these in my powered wheelchair |
| **Car Parking** | Opposite the railway station off Fishergate in the city centre |
| **Disabled toilet** | In the pavilion in Avenham Park. This is the modern building near to the river. The toilets are in the rear entrance to the Riverside Café |
| **Grid reference** | SD535290 |
| **Map** | OS Explorer Map 286 |

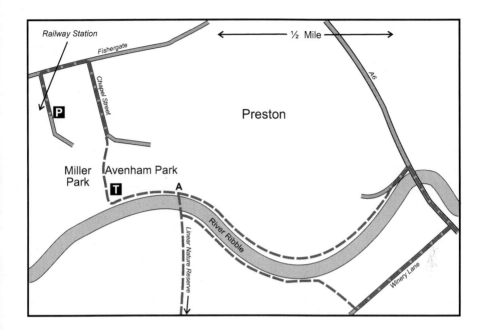

## Directions

From the car park retrace your route up past the railway station, turn right along Fishergate and take the third street on the right (Chapel Street). The entrance to Avenham Park is at the end of this street. Care needs to be taken further along here because of an absence of dropped kerbs, possibly requiring a short detour along the roadway at one point. As you enter the park head downhill, past the Japanese Garden and the pavilion (the modern building) to the banks of the River Ribble. Turn left and continue along the riverside. At point A you can either turn right to go over the bridge and along the track of the old railway, or you can carry straight on along the riverside. As mentioned above both paths have a short but very steep gradient at point A.

If you carry straight on along the riverside, you pass a children's playground and eventually come to a major road, the A6. Turn right along the A6, go over the wide bridge and take the third road (Winery Lane) on the right signposted 'Preston (Avenham Park) Penwortham' on a blue cyclists sign. Go along Winery Lane, taking care because, although there isn't much traffic along here, it does lack a pavement for much of its length. A few yards after the bridge and cattle grid take the path through a gate to the right. Follow this path through fields and then along the riverside back to the bridge which crosses the river at point A. Go under the bridge and then take the path up to the bridge round to the left. From here you can either turn right and explore the nature reserve along the old railway line or turn left to go through Avenham Park and back to the car.

## Points of Interest

Avenham Park and the adjacent Miller Park were built in the 1860s as a means of reducing unemployment in the town. At the time Lancashire was experiencing a cotton famine, because of the American Civil War, and this had serious consequences for the economy of cotton manufacturing towns like Preston.

Miller Park is situated to the right, as you enter the park from the city centre, as described above. It is more formal in layout than Avenham Park and is well worth exploring. A leaflet with a detailed map of both parks is available from the new pavilion building in Avenham Park.

*The riverside path in Avenham Park*

# 11. Clowbridge Reservoir, Burnley

A circular walk round a moorland reservoir with fine open views. There are semicircular kissing gates at each end of this walk which are accessible for most wheelchairs but unfortunately not for larger mobility scooters.

| | |
|---|---|
| **Distance** | Circular walk of 2 miles |
| **Path quality** | Level compacted stones/gravel throughout. There is a short slope down to the water's edge at the start of the walk, which is stony and rather bumpy, but the path quality improves beyond here and is fairly good for the rest of the walk. At the time of writing a bridge over a stream at point A has an awkward two to three inch step where the gravel in |
| **Car Parking** | Take the A682 from Burnley to Rawtenstall and after about 3 miles Clowbridge reservoir can be seen on your left. At the far end of the reservoir turn left just after the phone box and follow the track past the car park up to the disabled car park next to the sailing club |
| **Disabled toilet** | There is a public disabled toilet on the far side of the sailing club building from the disabled car park |
| **Grid reference** | SD824279 |
| **Map** | OS Explorer Map OL 21 |

## Directions
From the entrance to the disabled car park go down the short main entrance to the sailing club, and at the entrance to its car park take the

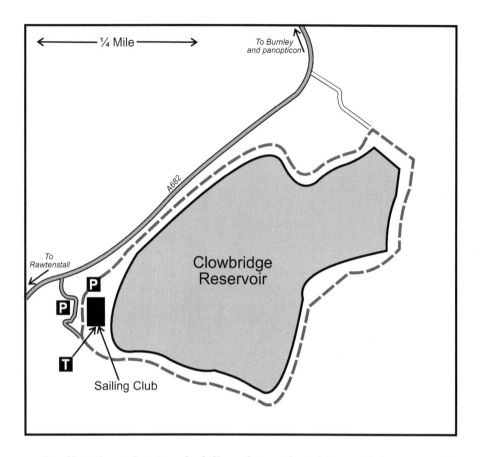

¼ Mile

To Burnley
and panopticon

A682

To
Rawtenstall

P

P

Clowbridge
Reservoir

T

Sailing Club

path off to the right. Simply follow this path right round the reservoir. At the far end of the reservoir, where you join a much wider track simply take the path off to your left to continue on round the reservoir.

## Points of Interest

About a mile north east of the reservoir, Crown Point Hill is the site of one of East Lancashire's four Panopticons. These are a series of sculptures funded by Lancashire Ecconomic Partnership in recent years. Panoptican literally means 'all seeing', and they are sited where they give a really good view over the surrounding area. The idea is that they symbolise the area's emergence from economic decline and look forward to a more prosperous future.

*The Singing Ringing Tree on Crown Point*

The one on Crown Point, 'The Singing Ringing Tree' was the winner of a National Award by the Royal Institute of British Architects in 2007. It makes a tuneful noise when the wind blows through it. You can only hear it when you are fairly close to it however.

The panopticon can be seen by turning right out of the Clowbridge Reservoir car park, back towards Burnley. After about 1½ miles the first road on the right, opposite 'The Bull' inn, leads up to the summit of Crown Point. The car park for the panopticon is just before the second cattle grid, on the left. A smooth path of compacted gravel with moderate gradients leads a few hundred yards from the car park across the moor to the sculpture.

Walk 20 gives details of another of the panopticons, some 12 miles away, near Wycoller.

# 12. Haworth Art Gallery, Accrington

An interesting and unusual small art gallery, a poignant war memorial and a pleasant cycle track in a small industrial town still trying to recover from the loss of the cotton trade and its former glory.

| | |
|---|---|
| **Distance** | 2½ miles circular walk |
| **Path quality** | Tarmac throughout. Gradients are easy to moderate except for Oak Hill Park beyond the war memorial, where the path descends steeply down to the main road |
| **Car Parking** | From Accrington take the A680 towards Haslingden and after about a mile turn right into Newton Drive at a brown tourist sign for 'Haworth Art Gallery'. Follow the brown signs down Hollins Lane to the Art Gallery on your right. There are 4 disabled parking spaces just in at the gate |
| **Disabled toilet** | In the Art Gallery |
| **Grid reference** | SD766271 |
| **Map** | OS Explorer Map 287 |

## Directions

Admission to the Art Gallery is free and the display of Tiffany glass should not be missed. The gardens are also pleasant to explore although they are on a considerable slope. For the walk itself take the path that leads away from the Art Gallery, just in at the gate, which runs parallel to Hollins Lane. At the end of the garden continue down Hollins Lane for a few hundred yards and Oak Hill Park is on the right just by the mini roundabout. It is necessary to detour off the pavement down part of Hollins Lane, due to a lack of dropped curbs, on a section where the pavement is raised up above the level of the

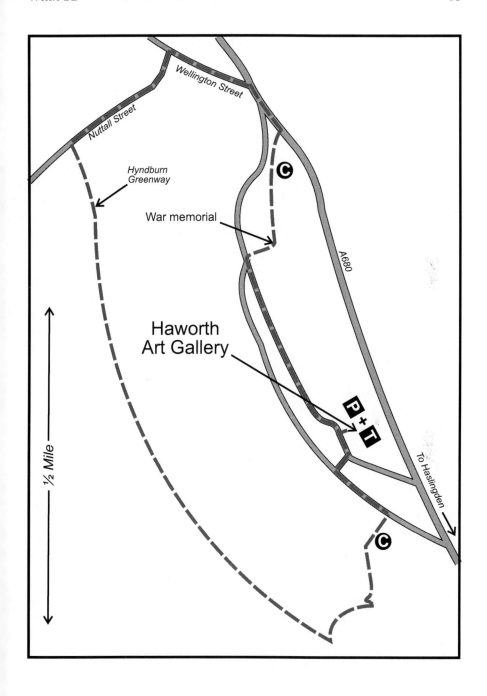

road, so extra care is needed. You will see the obelisk of the War Memorial straight in front of you from the park gates. You then take the main path down past the children's playground and through the park's main gates along the main road down to your left.

Turn left after about 130 yards down Wellington Street and, after another 250 yards turn left along Nuttall Street, just after a car park on the left. After another 300 yards or so the Hyndburn Greenway cycle path crosses Nuttall Street. This part of the walk between Oak Hill Park and Hyndburn Greenway is not the most picturesque part of East Lancashire, but it does give you a glimpse of the reality of parts of industrial Lancashire today. Go through the narrow cycle stile (I managed it OK in my powered wheelchair) and follow the track up through a long tree lined cutting and out into more open countryside. After nearly a mile take the tarmac path off to the left, and a little further on turn sharp left at a blue cycle route sign 'Hollins Technology College, Higher Baxenden'. Follow this path round past a children's playground and a school to join Hollins Lane. If you turn left, then first right, then left at the end, Howarth Art Gallery is just down here on the right. Note that there is no pavement for the final 100 yards of this route so great care is needed.

## Points of Interest
The Haworth Art Gallery, originally a private house built in 1909, was bequeathed to the people of Accrington, together with a collection of paintings, in 1920. The Tiffany glass collection was given to the town by local man Joseph Briggs. He emigrated to America in 1891, where he worked for the Tiffany Glass Company until it closed in 1933 due to a decrease in demand for Art Nouveau designs. He sent a selection of the remaining stock to Accrington and gave over 140 pieces to the local museum. These were later transferred to the Art Gallery. This is largest and most important collection of Tiffany Glass in the whole of Europe.

The 'Accrington Pals' was the nickname given to the town's battalion of volunteers that fought in the First World War. They were formed in response to an idea of Lord Kitchener's that they would get more volunteers if friends from the same area were allowed to fight together. At the Battle of the Somme more than half the battalion were either killed or wounded on the first day. In all 865 men from

Accrington were killed in the First World War. Their names are inscribed on the War Memorial in Oak Hill Park, together with the names of 173 Accrington men who were killed in the Second World War.

*Haworth Art Gallery*

# 13. Witton Country Park, Blackburn

A very pleasant country park on the outskirts of Blackburn, based in the grounds of the now demolished Witton House. There are wide open grassy spaces lined with trees and the one mile circular walk is on level well surfaced paths suitable for manual wheelchair users.

| | |
|---|---|
| **Distance** | This circular walk, including a visit to the Visitor Centre and lily pond, is about 1 mile |
| **Path quality** | The walk is mainly level and surfaced with either tarmac or good quality compacted gravel. There is a fairly gentle slope up to the Visitor Centre beyond point A |
| **Car Parking** | Take the A674 from Blackburn city centre towards Chorley and after about a mile Witton Country Park is signposted to the right on a brown tourist sign. There are 3 disabled parking spaces. There are a further 2 disabled parking spaces at the Visitor Centre but if you wish to use them there is a barrier across the access road which can be unlocked with a RADAR key |
| **Disabled toilet** | On the outside of the building to the right of the main Visitor Centre building. A RADAR key is required |
| **Grid reference** | SD662271 |
| **Map** | OS Explorer Map 287 |

## Directions
From the car park continue down the drive past the vehicle barrier, with the running track and children's playground on your right. The

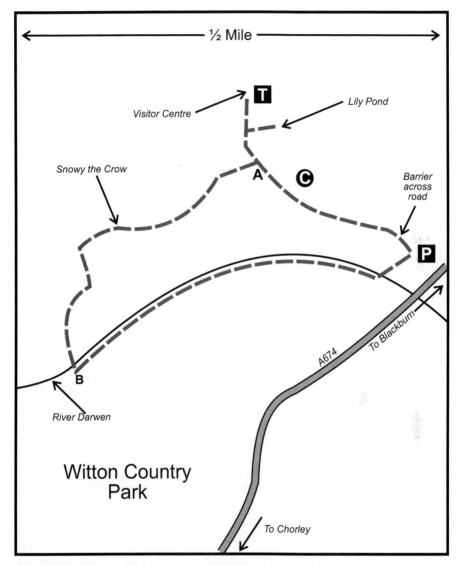

Visitor Centre is at the end of this drive through the large stone gateposts around the cobbled yard. A short distance before you reach these gateposts a path to the right leads to the lily pond. The delightful more formal gardens in this small area gives some idea of the former splendour of the Witton Estate.

Returning towards the car park, take the path to the right as you emerge from the trees signposted 'Pleasington, Snowy the Crow' (point A). As you skirt the trees at the edge of a large grassy area look out for the sculpture 'Snowy the Crow' on your right. Cross over the bridge over the River Darwen (point B) and turn left on a well-surfaced level path alongside the river then back over it on a delightful footbridge and hence back to the car park.

## Points of Interest

Witton House was built by the Fielden family in 1800 and they lived there for most of the nineteenth century. It was left empty for long periods after that however, and the house and the 480 acre estate was finally to sold to Blackburn Corporation in 1946. Unfortunately the house was in such a bad state of repair that it had to be demolished in 1952. The estate became a country park in 1973 and the Visitor Centre is located in the former stables and coach house.

All terrain mobility scooters called trampers are available to hire from the Visitor Centre. (See 'Points of Interest', Walk 29 for details). Routes are availble so that you can see much more of the country park than is accessible using a standard wheelchair or scooter.

*The lily pond*

# 14. Gawthorpe Hall, Padiham

A pleasant walk from the grounds of a stunning 17th century country house to a quiet country lane along the valley of the River Calder, on the very edge of industrial Lancashire.

## Directions
To see the Hall itself a path leads out of the far end of the car park. Turn right at the road then almost immediately left to continue down the drive. Where the drive swings round to the right a gate on the left gives access to the lawns at the rear of the Hall.

There is no admission charge for the grounds of Gawthorpe Hall and they are open throughout the year. Admission is charged for the Hall but it is not accessible for wheelchairs and is only open in the summer

*Gawthorpe Hall*

| Distance | 3½ miles from the car park to the gate across Grove Lane and back |
|---|---|
| Path quality | The car park and paths round the hall are of crushed stone and pebbles and they are fairly smooth and level, though not all are wheelchair accessible because of steps. The cobbled courtyard can be avoided because there is a smooth flagged path at the side of it. The walk itself is all tarmaced and mainly level but with a few gentle gradients. The disabled trail in Grove Lane Plantation has a good compressed cinder surface but it can be quite muddy in wet weather |
| Car Parking | Take the A671 from Padiham to Burnley and after about ⅓ of a mile Gawthorpe Hall is signposted on the left. Go through the entrance gates and continue down the drive past the training pitches for Burnley Football Club. The car park is signposted on the left 'Gawthorpe Hall Car Park' |
| Disabled toilet | From the car park continue down the drive for a little way taking an opening on the left (signpost 'To the tea-rooms') into a cobbled courtyard. Once in courtyard the first door on the left labelled 'Lavatories' leads to the disabled toilet, but this is only available when the hall itself is open for visitors. The nearest public disabled toilet is back in Padiham. Go up the hill from Padiham town centre towards Blackburn and Whalley. Bear left at the mini-roundabout and the toilet block is on the left just after the zebra crossing. A RADAR key is required |
| Grid reference | SD805340 |
| Map | OS Explorer Map 287 |

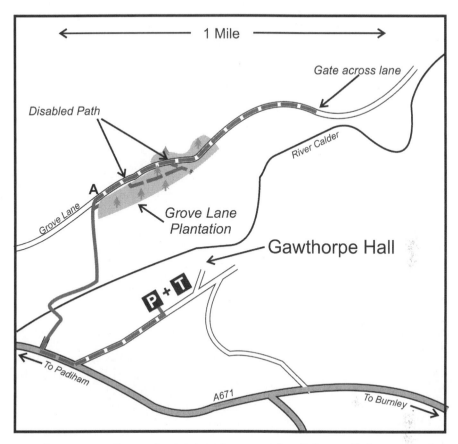

months. It is well worth visiting the outside of the Hall, however, for its stunning architecture and pleasant gardens.

For the walk itself, return down the drive to the main road, turn right towards Padiham and take the second right down Institute Street. At the bottom of the street take a footpath to the right alongside a grassed area. Continue over the footbridge over the river and turn immediately right following the factory fence, firstly alongside the river and then turning sharp left away from it, to eventually join a quiet tarmac lane at the start of Grove Lane Plantation (point A).

If you turn right along Grove Lane you can continue through the woods and then through farmland for about ½ a mile until you reach a gate across the track with a signpost that reads 'Private Road, Residents Only'. Return is by the same route. About 200 yards from point A, just at the end of a short stone wall, a disabled path to the right has been constructed leading through the trees to a viewpoint looking towards Gawthorpe Hall across the valley. From the lane go down a short gravel path and turn left. The 'trail of words' handrail (see Points of Interest below) can be seen along here. Returning from the viewpoint for a few yards a link path to the right brings you back onto the lane. As mentioned above this path can become muddy and in wet weather it might be advisable to avoid it and stay on the lane.

## Points of Interest

Gawthorpe Hall, built originally round a fourteenth century pele tower, was redesigned to its present splendour by Sir Charles Barry, the architect of the Houses of Parliament. The house was owned by the Kay-Shuttleworth family until 1970, when it was obtained by The National Trust, and it is full of its original antiques dating back to the English Civil War. Famous visitors to the Hall include Charlotte Brontë, a friend of the Kay-Shuttleworth family.

As you look across the valley from Gawthorpe Hall to Grove Lane Plantation it is hard to imagine the scene in the 1960s when the whole valley was subjected to open cast mining for coal. This is partly due to the Forest of Burnley project which was established to plant new woodland and to restore existing wood amounting to some 700 hectares in all, including the Grove Lane Plantation.

There is a trail for wheelchair users in Grove Lane Plantation along the track of the tramway (or 'Ginny Track') which was used to transport the coal. The handrail along the side of the disabled trail has carvings and poetry carved in it, the 'Trail of Words' which local children helped to create.

# 15. Towneley Park, Burnley

Towneley Hall and the parkland surrounding it have justifiably been described as 'The jewel in Burnley's crown'. There is something for everyone here and there is plenty to see and do in addition to the walk described below, which has been chosen for its fairly gentle gradients.

## Directions

From the long stay car park take a short path to the left near the river to the main drive that leads up to the Hall. Turn left at the far end of the main drive to go through the short stay car park and follow the signpost to 'Thanet Lee Woodland' taking the track up through the trees (past a 'No Entry' sign). Ignore the first path on your left but take a second path to the left just before the private gateway. Follow this path down through the woods ignoring any minor paths off to the left. Look out for wood sculptures in the trees along here. At the bottom of the hill the path swings round to the left in front of some football fields and crosses a stream on a bridge with a shallow step of about

*Towneley Hall*

| | |
|---|---|
| **Distance** | The suggested walk detailed below is about 1½ miles there and back. There are probably another couple of miles of wheelchair accessible paths in the wooded grounds behind the Hall |
| **Path quality** | The suggested walk paths have relatively easy gradients and are of tarmac in front of the Hall, and of fairly smooth compacted earth and pebbles through the woods. The paths in the grounds behind the Hall are mainly of tarmac but they are rather steep in places |
| **Car Parking** | Take the A671 from Burnley town centre towards Todmorden and after about ½ mile 'Towneley Hall' is signposted on the left on a brown tourist sign, shortly after a mini-roundabout. Continue along the drive for about ½ mile then fork left and follow signs to the long stay car park. There are 8 disabled parking spaces. Note: If you carry straight on instead of taking the left fork (signposted 'short stay car park'), there is limited parking in front of the Hall with a further 8 disabled parking spaces but these are likely to be full when it is busy. Disabled parking is allowed here for three hours |
| **Disabled toilet** | In the circular building on the car park. There is also one in the Hall's entrance, available when the Hall is open |
| **Grid reference** | SD858313 |
| **Map** | OS Explorer Map OL21 |

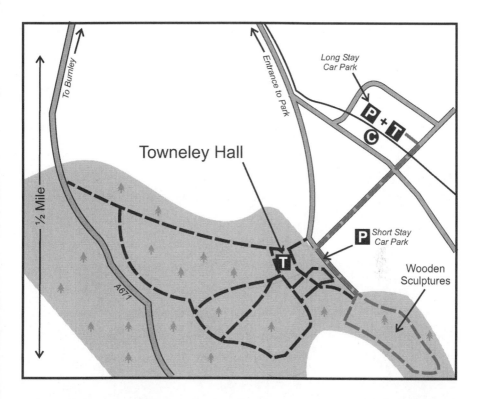

an inch and a half, before rejoining the track. Hence turn right and retrace your steps back to the car park.

From the short stay car park in front of the Hall, a gate at the right leads to the Hall and the network of paths in its grounds. The black dotted lines on the map above shows the approximate layout of the major paths behind the Hall. Some of these paths are rather steep.

## Points of Interest

The Towneleys are a prominent local family who have lived on this site from the 13th century and the present Hall dates from the 14th and 16th centuries, with major renovations in the 18th century.

In 1902 Burnley Borough Council bought the Hall and its grounds and established an impressive art gallery and a museum of local history, together with superb grounds where they built woodland walks, a golf

course and several football fields. More recently, an excellent
children's playground, a sculpture trail and a café have been added.
The children's playground is over the river from the main car park.

Towneley Park was bought for the people of Burnley and is known
locally as 'the jewel in Burnley's crown'. There is an admission charge
for the Hall but Burnley residents are admitted free of charge. Entry
to the grounds is free for everyone.

*The Avenue looking from in front of the Hall towards the long-stay car park*

# 16. Burnley, Hurstwood

This walk affords easy access onto the surrounding moorland, with long distance views of typical Pennine scenery. Hurstwood is a tiny village of charming old cottages that nestle in a hollow besides the infant river Brun, from which Burnley gets its name.

| | |
|---|---|
| **Distance** | 1½ miles there and back |
| **Path quality** | The first ¼ mile, up through the trees as far as the reservoir, is of tarmac but with a moderate uphill gradient. Beyond here the moorland track is level with a fairly good surface |
| **Car Parking** | From the village of Worsthorne, situated a couple of miles East of Burnley, take the road South out of the village (Salterford Lane) for about ½ mile. The hamlet of Hurstwood is signposted to the left down Hurstwood Lane. As you enter Hurstwood continue straight on, on a wide pebbled track which leads to the car park |
| **Disabled toilet** | The nearest one is at Towneley Park about 2½ miles away. From Hurstwood turn left at the end of Hurstwood Lane then right at the end of Salterford Lane towards Burnley. After about ½ mile take the third road on the left down Springwood Road. Keep left at the 20 mph sign and follow the road down through the golf course, going round to the right opposite the garden centre. There is a car park on the left with 8 disabled parking spaces and a circular building which houses the disabled toilet |
| **Grid reference** | SD883313 |
| **Map** | OS Explorer Map OL21 |

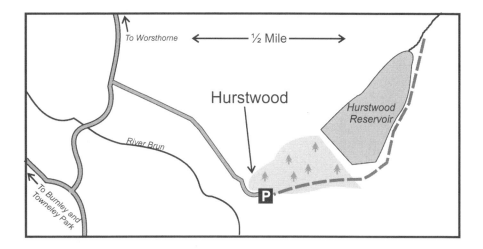

## Directions

The path starts from the top corner of the car park by an information board and joins a tarmac path where you turn right uphill through the trees. Go straight on through the gate by the corner of the reservoir and continue straight on for about half a mile until a

*Hurstwood Reservoir and surrounding moor land*

'Burnley Way' signpost is reached. Beyond here the path becomes too rough for wheelchairs so it is necessary to retrace your steps back to the car park.

Points of Interest
The track along the side of the reservoir is a small section of the Pennine Bridleway, a long distance path for walkers, cyclists and horse riders which, when it is finally completed, will run for some 350 miles from Derbyshire to Northumberland. The idea for the bridle way came from Mary Towneley, whose relatives originated from nearby Towneley Hall (see directions for 'disabled toilet' above). She pioneered the route on horseback in 1986 and a 47 mile section in this area, The Mary Towneley Loop, was opened in 2002.

# 17. Spring Wood, Whalley

A short walk through ancient woodland that is home to an impressive variety of wildlife. The extensive display of bluebells is a delight in the springtime. If you have time a visit to nearby Whalley Abbey is well worthwhile. (see 'Points of Interest' below)

| | |
|---|---|
| **Distance** | The low mobility path is just under ½ mile there and back. The circular path is a little over ½ mile |
| **Path quality** | The car park is tarmaced. The low mobility path slopes very gently and has a fairly good surface of crushed stone/ fine pebbles. The circular path is somewhat rougher. It rises steadily up to point A and then descends similarly on the return leg back to the car park. The path is uneven and bumpy in places but I didn't find it too bad in my fairly lightweight electric wheelchair |
| **Car Parking** | Turn right off the A671 Burnley to Whalley road at the next set of traffic lights after its junction with the A680 to Great Harwood. There are 3 disabled parking spaces in the first car parking area and a further one near the ramp to the low mobility path in the adjacent car parking area |
| **Disabled toilet** | On the car park. A RADAR key is required |
| **Grid reference** | SD741361 |
| **Map** | OS Explorer Map 287 |

## Directions
The walk starts from the far left-hand corner of the second car parking area up a fairly short access ramp to join the low mobility

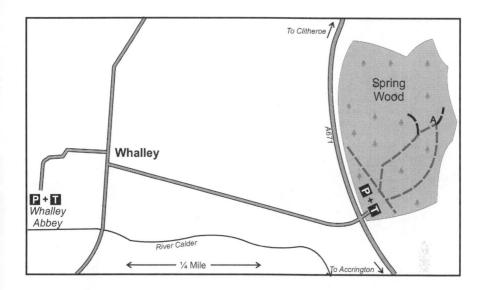

trail. The majority of the trail, is to the left and there are one or two short loops to the right leading to information boards along the way. Return is by the same route and it is possible to continue a short way past the access ramp in the other direction.

For the Circular walk take the access ramp from the car park, turn left and then take the next path on the right. Continue uphill and bear right near a small sunken pond. At the next junction turn sharply right (point A) to start the descent back to the car park.

Note that there are several other paths in Spring Wood, but if you try to follow them you'll soon find that they are far too rough for most wheelchairs and scooters.

## Points of Interest
There is a small Information Centre in part of the toilet block with details about the site and its wildlife. Spring Wood is classed as ancient woodland. It was once owned by Whalley Abbey and it has remained virtually unchanged for several hundred years except for the planting of rhododendron in the 19th century. Cistercian monks moved from Stanlow in Cheshire to Whalley in 1296 where they built an Abbey which survived until the dissolution of the Monasteries in 1536.

*Ruins of Whalley Abbey from the riverside path*

The ruins of Whalley Abbey, are about ½ mile away and they are well worth visiting. From the car park go straight on through the traffic lights and down the hill to the mini-roundabout. Turn right and then first left, round the DeLacey Arms, down Church Lane. Follow the road past the church and the school and bear left and then straight on through the arched gateway of Whalley Abbey into the courtyard car park. This courtyard is of rough cobbles but it's not too bad in a wheelchair if you can avoid the worst of the bumps.

There is a disabled toilet in one corner of the courtyard, next to an excellent, small Information Centre with models of the Abbey and displays about its history. Next to this is a pleasant café/tearoom which in turn leads through to a gift shop where tickets can be purchased for a visit to the Abbey ruins themselves. Some of the paths around the ruins are not too rough, and they are mostly level, but there are some steps and so not all the paths are accessible for wheelchairs.

However, there is an alternative short riverside walk (about ¹/₃ mile there and back) which takes you down the side of the Abbey ruins. From the courtyard go through a gateway in one corner signposted 'Extra Car Park'. This leads down to the banks of the river Calder where you can explore for a short way in either direction.

# 18. Barley Picnic Site

Two delightful walks in a superb rural setting from the unspoilt village of Barley, right at the foot of Pendle Hill.

| | |
|---|---|
| **Distance** | The walk downstream is 1¼ miles in total. The walk upstream is also about 1¼ miles there and back |
| **Path quality** | The first half of the walk down stream is bumpy in places, particularly the cobbled street at Narrowgates. The path beyond here is somewhat stony and bumpy in places and although it is tarmaced the hill at Whitehough up to the main road is very steep. The path upstream is tarmaced as far as Ogden reservoir, but again the last 200 yards rising up to the top of the reservoir dam is also very steep, and at the time of writing the tarmac on this hill has deep potholes in places so extra care is needed. The track alongside the reservoir is essentially fairly smooth and most potholes can be avoided |
| **Car Parking** | In the centre of the village at the start of the road to Roughlee |
| **Disabled toilet** | On the car park. A RADAR key is required |
| **Grid reference** | SD824403 |
| **Map** | OS Explorer Map OL21 |

## Directions

For the walk downstream, a short narrow path from the side of the car park away from the toilet block leads to an unmade road. Turn left

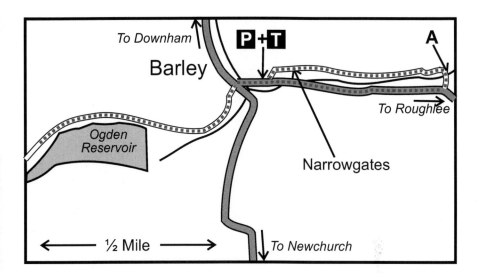

and continue down the cobbled street of the hamlet of Narrowgates. Continue past the mill-workers cottages to go through a gate leading to a rather bumpy path besides a large stream (Pendle Water).

After about ½ mile, in the hamlet of Whitehough, the path joins a quiet tarmac road which swings over the stream to the right and climbs very steeply uphill to join the road leading to Roughlee. Turn right here and follow the pavement back to the car park.

For the walk upstream, turn right at the car park's entrance, and at the road junction cross the road and go down the side of the village hall signposted 'To Barley Green'. Follow this lane round to the left and go through the gateway with a United Utilities sign 'Private Road No Public Vehicular Access'. Continue on past the water treatment plant on your right, up the hill and straight on by the side of the reservoir until a cattle grid is reached. There is little point continuing further as the track soon climbs steeply uphill again and then deteriorates into a rough path.

## Points of Interest
There are records of Barley as an agricultural village going back to the 13th century. Incomes in the village were supplemented by a cottage textile industry and this led to two cotton mills being built in the

village early in the 19th century. There was one at Narrowgates, now a private residence, near the start of the walk downstream from the car park. You can get a glimpse of what life must have been like for the cotton workers as you walk down the cobbled street between their old cottages. The second mill was situated near the walk, upstream on the site of the water treatment plant. This mill was destroyed by a flood in 1880. The Ogden reservoirs a short distance up the valley were built just before the First World War.

Pendle Hill is the highest point in this area and its distinctive shape can be seen for miles around in all directions. In 1652 George Fox climbed Pendle Hill. As he looked out at the view across the Lancashire plain to the coast, he reported afterwards that God spoke to him in a vision. This experience lead to the foundation of the Quaker Society of Friends.

Perhaps more famously is the fact that the 'Pendle Witches' came from this area. They were allegedly responsible for several murders in the

*Narrowgates with the old cotton mill at the end of the street*

*Pendle Hill from the Newchurch to Barley Road*

area and ten of them were hanged for witchcraft in 1612. The village of Newchurch, ¾ miles away, has a gift shop devoted to the subject called 'Witches Galore', and the village Church has a carving on its tower called 'the eye of God' whose purpose was to protect the parishioners from witchcraft. Apparently the Pendle Witches raided the graveyard for bones which they used in their spells. Local legend has it that the witches fly over Pendle Hill at halloween and to this day crowds of local people climb the hill on halloween night. Further information on the Pendle Witches can be found at The Pendle Heritage Centre (see 'Points of Interest', Walk 20).

# 19. Barrowford Locks

This is a pleasant canal-side walk right on the edge of industrial Lancashire. I never fail to be amazed at the skill and determination of the canal engineers who managed to build this canal, right over the Pennine Hills, using the most basic of tools and equipment.

| Distance | 2¾ miles there and back |
| --- | --- |
| Path quality | Tarmac throughout. The path is mostly level with fairly easy gradients up past the locks and approaching the tunnel |
| Car Parking | From Junction 13 of the M65 take the A682 towards Gisburn and after nearly a mile turn right over the bridge to Colne. Pass Pendle Heritage centre on your right and then after about ¹/₃ mile take the first right, just over a modern bridge then turn right again. The car park is a few yards down this road on the right |
| Disabled toilet | The nearest public one is back in Barrowford, at the side of the A682 about ¾ mile away, but parking near it is not easy. There is one at Pendle Heritage Centre, accessed through the tea-rooms, and when the bowling greens are in use in Barrowford Park, adjacent to the Heritage Centre, there is one accessed from the outside of the bowling pavilion |
| Grid reference | SD869397 |
| Map | OS Explorer Map OL21 |

## Directions

From the car park the path leads to the canal bank. It crosses under the road bridge by the side of a lock then opens out onto the tarmac

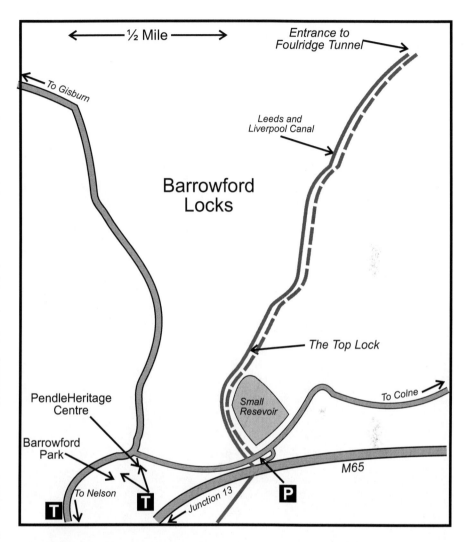

access road for the lock-keepers cottage by the top lock. Before the top lock however there is a locked gate across this road with a stile at the side designed for cyclists. I managed to get through this without any difficulty using a standard size powered wheelchair.

The path continues beside the canal up to the top level, where a colourful collection of boats are moored, and on under a couple of bridges to the approach to the tunnel. A narrow muddy path right by the water's edge starts here but it is advisable to stay on the tarmac path up through the trees, to emerge right above the mouth of the tunnel. There is a short rough footpath leading back to the fence overlooking the tunnel. If you can negotiate this you will be rewarded by a much better view. Return is by the same route.

## Points of Interest

The Leeds and Liverpool canal is 127 miles long and has 91 locks to raise it up over the Pennines and down the other side. The canal took 46 years to build and was completed in 1816.The highest point of the canal is at the top of the Barrowford locks. It is fed by several reservoirs in the area because a lot of water is needed to keep the canal full. Every time a boat passes through a lock either up or down, a lock-full of water is transferred to the lower level. The Foulridge tunnel is nearly a mile long. It hit the headlines in 1912 when a cow fell into the canal at the Barrowford end of the tunnel and for some

*Pendle Heritage Centre*

unknown reason swam all the was through it. She was rescued in Foulridge and revived with alcohol.

Pendle Heritage Centre, just ¹/₃ mile back along the road from the car park, is well worth a visit. There is a museum, art gallery, gift shop and tourist information centre devoted to the local area including information about the Pendle Witches (see also 'Points of Interest', Walk 19). There is a Cruck-framed barn, an 18th century walled garden and a tea-room specialising in Lancashire dishes. The centre has a disabled toilet and a wheelchair is also available. Adjacent to Pendle Heritage Centre, the very pleasant Barrowford Park has mostly wheelchair accessible paths and a children's playground. There is a car park at the Heritage Centre with 3 disabled spaces and an overflow car park on the other side of the road opposite the Heritage Centre.

# 20. Wycoller Country Park

Wycoller is a small Pennine village tucked away in a secluded valley that has remained virtually unchanged for hundreds of years. It has remained to this day a small community of hill farmers and the country park itself is in fact essentially working farmland. The ruins of its Hall have literary connections to the Brontë sisters but its history goes much further back than this as its ancient footbridges will testify.

## Directions

From the right-hand corner of the car park near the road a path running besides the road leads down into the village. Although it is tarmaced there are one or two steep and awkward sections on this path. The path joins the road and you simply follow it round into the village until you reach a ford over Wycoller Beck. Turn right here alongside the beck and take a path to the right just past the clapper bridge. This path has been specially constructed for wheelchairs and leads past some interesting willow sculptures to a bridge over the beck a little higher upstream. Cross the bridge and if you turn right at this point (point A), you come to the ancient clam bridge (see 'Points of Interest' below).

A strange elliptical structure, the panopticon 'Atom' can be seen on the hill up to the left as you approach the clam bridge. It is possible to continue further up this track if you wish until a point is reached where the track divides. The various footpaths become inaccessible for wheelchairs a little beyond this point.

Returning to point A and continuing on past it, the aisled barn and the ruins of Wycoller Hall are a little way down on the right and are well worth exploring. Return is by the same route.

## Points of Interest

The 16th century Wycoller Hall, which only became derilict at the start of the 20 th century, was well known to Charlotte Brontë, who lived just a few miles away at Haworth. It is believed that 'Ferndean Manor' in the novel *Jane Eyre* was based on Wycoller Hall.

| Distance | About 2 miles there and back |
|---|---|
| Path quality | Tarmac down to the village and along the disabled path to the bridge over the river. The path at the other side of the river is an unsurfaced farm track that is not too rough for wheelchairs if you can avoid the potholes. There is a moderate gradient down to the village, otherwise paths are mostly level. Access to the aisled barn from the main track is cobbled and if you wish to inspect the ruins of Wycoller Hall at close quarters it is necessary to go across a grassy area |
| Car Parking | From the Colne end of the M65 take the A6068 towards Keighley and immediately after the third roundabout turn right towards Trawden on the B6250. Wycoller Country Park is signposted from here on brown tourist signs. You continue down the B5250 for 1¼ miles then turn very sharply left onto Keighley road. Go up the hill and take the second turn to the right, signposted 'Wycoller Country Park' on a brown sign. The car park is about ½ a mile down on the right. Disabled badge holders are allowed to continue on and park in the village, either by the ford or at the side of the aisled barn, but space is very limited |
| Disabled toilet | Behind the aisled barn |
| Grid reference | SD926395 |
| Map | OS Explorer Map OL21 |

The adjacent aisled barn, built in 1630, is an important grade II listed building, which has more recently won architectural awards for the sympathetic way it has been converted into a fully wheelchair

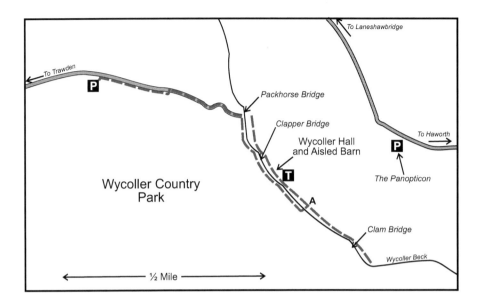

accessible information centre. The design of the barn suggests a change in agricultural use from keeping animals to growing crops, due to rapid increases in the price of cereals in the latter part of the 16th century. During the 17th century however, deterioration in the climate forced a return to stock rearing as the main agricultural activity in the area.

The foot bridges that cross the stream at Wycoller are of very different designs. The mis-shaped pack-horse bridge just downstream of the ford in the village, looks as though it is about to collapse, when in fact it has withstood the test of time since the 13th century.

The next bridge upstream, the clapper bridge, dates from the late 18th century and was built for weavers to take their cloth to the field behind the hall to stretch it out on tenter-hooks to dry.

The Clam Bridge, the furthest footbridge, some way upstream from the village, is formed from a single slab of stone and is thought to date from the iron age. It was swept away and broken by floods in 1989 and in 1990, but has since been repaired.

Wycoller Country Park is also the site of one of East Lancashire's four panopticon sculptures. See 'Points of Interest' for Walk 11 for more details on the panopticon project. The Wycoller panopticon, 'Atom' was completed in 2006. It combines stunning views over the surrounding countryside, with shelter from which to enjoy these views.

The panopticon is not accessible from this walk by wheelchair. It is necessary to return to the car, turn left out of the car park, then right at the T-junction and first right again after about 100 yards Follow this road for about 1 mile, turn right at the T-junction and the car park for Wycoller Country Park is in about 1¼ miles on the right. A gravel path leads from the car park to the sculpture.

*The packhorse bridge*

# 21. Lytham Promenade

This is the first of the Fylde Coast Walks. (See the 'An Overview of the Fylde Coast' on page 7 for further details). Lytham has a large proportion of retirement homes and this level tarmac route away from the traffic is popular with its residents.

| | |
|---|---|
| Distance | 3 miles return from the windmill to the White Church. plus any detour around Lowther gardens |
| Path quality | Level tarmac throughout |
| Car Parking | There are two Car Parks on Lytham Green (the coastal stretch of the A584 at Lytham) just North of the windmill. The first one has 3 disabled spaces and the other has 4 disabled spaces. There is also a car park at Lowther Gardens with 6 disabled spaces |
| Disabled toilet | There is a disabled toilet in a low building just south of the Windmill and one on the car park at Lowther Gardens. Both require a RADAR key (or 20p) |
| Grid reference | SD368270 |
| Map | OS Explorer Map 286 |

## Directions
From one of the car parks on Lytham Green simply follow the path on the seaward side of the Green. It is just a short distance to the South

*The windmill on Lytham Green*

past the lifeboat station to Lytham's famous windmill, and to the North the path continues on past the end of the Green. If you take the last path to the right, just before the end of the Green, you can cross the road and turn back right for a short distance for a very pleasant detour into Lowther Gardens.

Continuing on past the end of the Green, the path follows the sea wall through an area of scrubland until it joins the Inner Promenade, near to the White Church. Return is by the same route. If you decide to continue along the Inner Promenade around the bay for another ¹/₃ of a mile however you will arrive at the car park at Fairhaven Lake, which is the start of Walk 24.

## Points of Interest
The windmill was built in 1805 and operated until 1919 when it was destroyed by fire in a gale. Apparently the wind was so powerful that

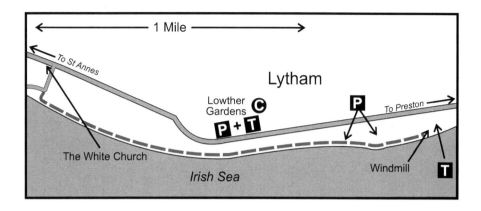

it turned the sails despite the brake being engaged. This caused sparks which set the woodwork alight. It was given to the local council in a derelict state and, in 1989, it was fully restored by Fylde Borough Council. The windmill is open to the public free of charge in the Summer months and houses exhibitions on the history and workings of the mill .

The White Church was built in 1912 by Lytham Congregational Church. They certainly realised their aim of building a Church that would be 'a distinctive architectural feature' in the area. It was built by a Blackburn firm of Architects in a Byzantine style using white faced bricks. Apparently the dome is suspended by wires and is still of interest today to architects and structural engineers. The Church became part of The United Reformed Church in 1972.

# 22. Fairhaven Lake, Lytham

This is the second of the Fylde Coast Walks. (See 'An Overview of the Fylde Coast' on page 7 for further details). This walk differs from the others in that it consists of a circular walk round a large artificial but well established lake which is home to a variety of water fowl. There is a small shop and Visitor Centre for the Royal Society for the Protection of Birds by the water's edge towards the end of this walk.

| | |
|---|---|
| **Distance** | Circular walk of a little over 1 mile |
| **Path quality** | Tarmac throughout. There is a fairly gentle slope from both the south and the north car parks down to the water's edge. Otherwise paths are level |
| **Car Parking** | Travelling from Lytham to Blackpool on the A584, turn left at the White Church down Ansdell Road South about a mile from the centre of Lytham. Follow the road round along the Inner Promenade and Fairhaven Lake is on the left in about ¼ of a mile. There are three car parks round Fairhaven Lake. One to the South with 6 disabled spaces (three at each end), one half way along on the road side with 4 disabled spaces, and one to the north with 4 disabled spaces. The directions below start from the car park at the south but you could start this circular walk from any point |
| **Disabled toilet** | By the water's edge behind the ice cream cabin at the entrance to the south car park. A RADAR key (or 20p) is required |
| **Grid reference** | SD344274 |
| **Map** | OS Explorer Map 286 |

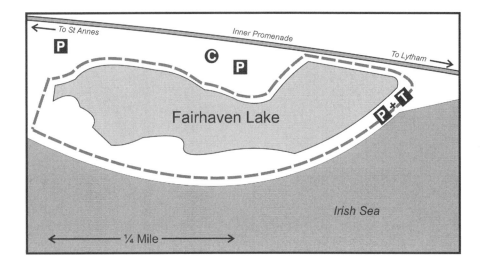

## Directions
From your parking place on the South car park continue on through this long curved car park to join a path along the sea wall. This path eventually turns sharply inland through a short cutting through the sand dunes to emerge in the north car park. You can take either of two paths from this car park down to the water's edge. If you take the first one turn almost immediately left to continue round the lake. It is joined by the second path from the car park a little further on. This second path is more straight-forward and possibly a little easier. The path continues on round the lake, past parkland with various visitor attractions such as a children's playground and boat hire, and returns to the south car park up an incline next to the toilet block.

## Points of Interest
Fairhaven Lake was built at the end of the nineteenth century from a natural harbour between two banks of stones, where local fishermen used to moor their boats. It is a salt water lake where annual boat regattas were held from 1900 to the 1960s. The lake is also important for the wildfowl that it attracts. The mudflats of the nearby Ribble Estuary are important winter feeding grounds for these birds. More information on this is available from the RSPB Visitor Centre at the lakeside.

*Fairhaven Lake from the South Car Park*

# 23. St Anne's Promenade

This is the third of the Fylde Coast Walks. (See 'An Overview of the Fylde Coast' on page 7 for further details). St Annes is a resort catering for mainly younger families in the Great British seaside holiday tradition. If this traditional seaside experience is not really your thing, St Annes is a good way of gently preparing yourself for the shock to the system that awaits you further north in Blackpool itself!

| | |
|---|---|
| **Distance** | About 1¼ to 1½ miles including detours to see the various features in the ornamental gardens |
| **Path quality** | Virtually level tarmac throughout |
| **Car Parking** | Driving North along Lytham's Inner Promenade past Fairhaven Lake (see Walk 24), Fairhaven Road car park is on the left at the end of the grassy scrubland about 1 mile past Fairhaven Lake. There are 4 disabled parking spaces. There is a large car park further along the road just after the pier with 3 disabled parking spaces at each end |
| **Disabled toilet** | At the car park entrance.  Also in the ornamental gardens just South of the pier. A RADAR key (or 20p) is required at both these toilets |
| **Grid reference** | SD324280 |
| **Map** | OS Explorer Map 286 |

## Directions

From the car park entrance take the path to the north along the promenade,  turning left after about 100 yards down a path alongside a miniature train track which runs round a mini-golf course. This path follows the sea wall past the lifeboat station and a small boating lake

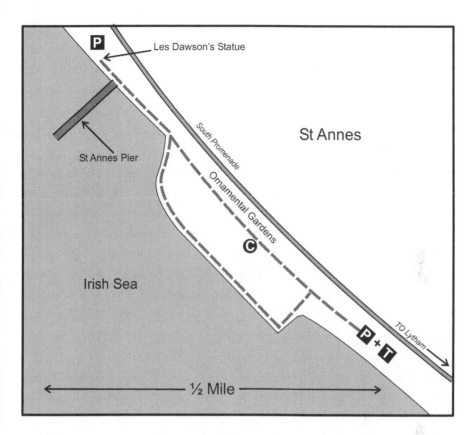

and on as far as the St Annes pier. Beyond the pier there is a small garden with a statue of the comedian Les Dawson. There is little point in continuing further, however, as the promenade ends and there is only a car park beyond here. If you return to the car park by the broad promenade instead of following the sea wall, there are a series of delightful ornamental gardens to explore on your left, including am impressive artificial waterfall where the path actually passes underneath it.

## Points of Interest

St Annes was a planned seaside resort which was built in the last quarter of the nineteenth century to cater for the Lancashire mill workers. Although it has been modernised since then it still retains much of its Victorian character and charm to this day.

The beach to the north of St Annes was used for sand-yachting until 2002 when a fatal accident occurred to a visitor on the beach. Sand yachting has now been replaced by kite-flying events on the beach as the main sporting activity.

*The waterfall in the ornamental gardens*

# 24. Blackpool Tower

This walk provides a convenient place to park to visit Blackpool's attractions, including the iconic Blackpool Tower. The tower is wheelchair accessible, except for the stairs right at the top, but admission is quite expensive because it includes the other attractions that are available at the Tower entertainment complex.

| | |
|---|---|
| **Distance** | 2½ miles there and back. The cliff-top path to Bispham is up to 3 miles return |
| **Path quality** | Apart from slopes down to the lower promenade there is level tarmac throughout |
| **Car Parking** | Continue along the promenade north of the Tower and turn right at the round-about at Gynn Square. The car park is on the left at the start of Warbreck Hill Road. There are 4 disabled parking spaces |
| **Disabled toilet** | Near the roundabout at the start of the walk. A RADAR key (or 20p) is required |
| **Grid reference** | SD307380 |
| **Map** | OS Explorer Map 286 |

## Directions

From the car park cross the road near to the roundabout to reach the promenade. There are dropped kerbs here but the road is very busy so great care is needed. Turn left to go past the toilets and take a slope to the right, back on yourself, to go down to the lower promenade. This continues southwards along the sea wall and eventually rises up

*Blackpool Tower from the lower promenade*

a slope to the entrance to the North Pier. Continue past this for 100 yards or so then cross the tram tracks and road at one of the crossing points along here. You are now on the 'Golden Mile' part of the promenade, with its many attractions to explore. Wheelchair access to Blackpool Tower itself is round the back of the building. Return is by the same route.

The walk can be extended by going north from point A, past some gardens, and then on to a fine cliff-top path as far as Norbreck tram station, again returning by the same route

## Points of Interest
Blackpool Tower was built as a tourist attraction in 1894 as a result of a visit to the Eiffel Tower in Paris by John Bickerstaffe, the mayor of Blackpool. It cost over £290,000 pounds to build and some five million bricks, and 2,500 tonnes of iron were used in its construction. It is

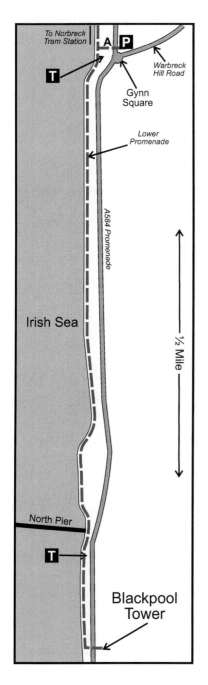

518 feet high and is designed in such a way that if it were ever to collapse it would fall into the sea. In 1891 a time capsule was buried beneath its foundations. During the first thirty years of its life it was not painted properly, with the result that the ironwork corroded badly and it had to be completely rebuilt. It remained in the ownership of the Bickerstaffe family until 1964 and is now owned by Leisure Parcs Ltd.

# 25. Wyre Estuary Country Park, Thornton

As you take in the wide open horizons of the Wyre Estuary it's hard to believe how close the Fylde Coast's urban sprawl really is. This is however a dog walker's paradise that hasn't gone unnoticed by the locals.

| Distance | About 2 miles |
|---|---|
| Path quality | The path is mainly level throughout with quite a good compacted pebbly surface along the shore. At the start of this section there is a sign, however, that warns that the path can be flooded at extreme high tide. At point A, where the route turns inland, there is a rough track with numerous potholes of perhaps 200 yards to be negotiated before reaching Underbank Road. The rest of the walk is on tarmac roads and pavements |
| Car Parking | Travelling towards Fleetwood on the A585, take the B5412 at the roundabout just after the River Wyre Hotel. Follow the signs for 'Stanah Picnic Site' to the car park in front of the Visitor Centre. There are five disabled parking spaces and picnic tables nearby |
| Disabled toilet | At the Visitor Centre. RADAR key required |
| Grid reference | SD355430 |
| Map | OS Explorer Map 296 |

## Directions
From the car park, walk towards the shore to the right and follow the path signposted 'Riverside Path to Cockle Hall and Skipool'. Continue

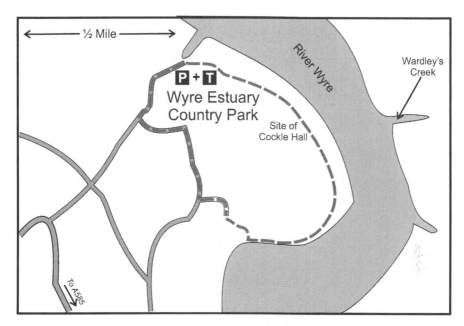

on for about a mile then take a track to the right signposted 'Underbank Road'. At the end of the track turn right down Underbank Road and continue on to the junction with River Road. Turn right again and hence return to the car park.

## Points of Interest

About ½ mile from the start of the walk there are a couple of information boards at Cockle Hall picnic site. Cockle Hall, now demolished, was once the home of a ferry man who carried people across the river to Wardley's Creek on the opposite bank. In the 18th century Wardle's Creek was a

*The riverside path*

major port of North West England, rivalling the port of Liverpool. It was also a ship building centre and, apparently, when its biggest ever ship was built in the 1830s it caused such a big wave that several hundred spectators on the opposite bank of the river were soaked!

# 26. Fleetwood Promenade

A fine sandy beach on a level tarmac path well away from the noise of traffic. Despite being near the centre of Fleetwood there is a sense of splendid isolation as you travel between the low sand dunes.

| Distance | Circular walk of 2 miles |
|---|---|
| Path quality | Level tarmac throughout except for the short link path from the outer promenade to the road which is unsurfaced but not too rough |
| Car Parking | From the centre of Fleetwood take the coast road to the left (The Esplanade) and after a few hundred yards the car park is on the right next to the Marine Hall and opposite a small park on the left. There are 4 disabled parking spaces and a further 4 at the far end of the car park nearer to the town centre and the children's playground |
| Disabled toilet | On the car park at the side of the Marine Hall. Also just up Beach Road on right at the far end of the walk |
| Grid reference | SD334483 |
| Map | OS Explorer Map 296 |

## Directions

From the car park head towards the sea to turn left along the outer promenade. After nearly a mile take a path to the left opposite a concrete ramp onto the beach. There is a roughly painted sign 'café' on a concrete wall at this point. Take this path down to the road and return along the pavement past the boating lake and gardens and hence back to the car park. If you turn right in the car park and go round to the far end a short path leads up to the children's playground.

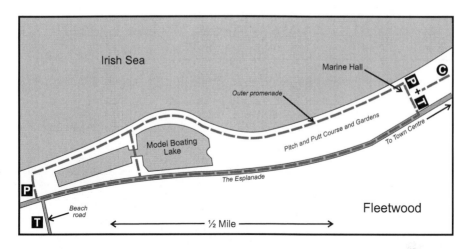

*The pavement past the model boating lake*

# 27. Millennium Green, Garstang

A delightful riverside walk in typical Lancashire countryside on the edge of the attractive small town of Garstang, with superb views of the Bowland Fells in the distance. This walk has the added advantage of literally passing right through the middle of a most interesting and unusual flood defence system.

| | |
|---|---|
| **Distance** | $1^2/_3$ miles return. The walk from the flood barrier towards Greenhalgh Castle is about $^2/_3$ mile return |
| **Path quality** | Good quality compacted crushed stone throughout. Paths are mainly level except for the access ramps over the flood barrier, which are of moderate gradient. The path towards Greenhalgh Castle has fairly easy gradients |
| **Car Parking** | Travelling South on the A6 fork left on the B6430, signposted 'Garstang'. After about ¾ mile turn left at a mini-roundabout into the car park. There are 17 disabled parking spaces |
| **Disabled toilet** | On the car park. A RADAR key is required |
| **Grid reference** | SD493454 |
| **Map** | OS Explorer Map 296 |

## Directions

From the car park take the path past the toilets towards the river, turn left and follow the riverside path round the edge of the cricket pitch. Go under the bridge and bear left up the access path to the top of the flood barrier (point A). Cross the concrete road and take the path down to the right, then through the gate at the bottom to continue along the riverside path. Continue along this path for about ½ mile to

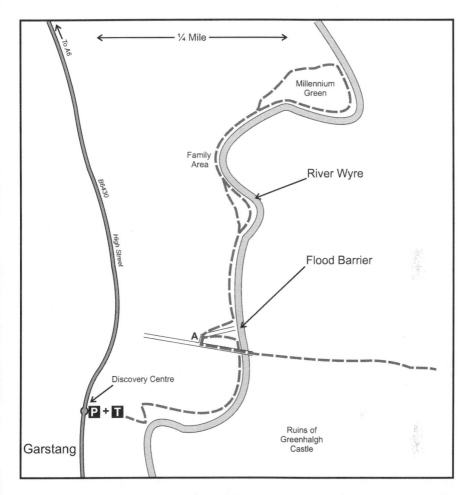

where the path loops round to the left to enable you to do a circuit of the Millennium Green. Return is by the same route.

The path beyond the flood barrier is in the flood basin (see Points of Interest below). If you look out for pieces of driftwood several feet up in the trees at the side of the path you will get some idea of the depth of water this basin can hold. Also, there are sculptures and information boards along the way. A new family area is also being developed along here, which will be a picnic area and a dog free zone for children to play in.

To go on the old railway track towards Greenhalgh Castle, turn right at point A along the concrete roadway on the top of the flood barrier. After a few yards turn left to go over the bridge and continue along this path until a wooden kissing gate is reached, which at the time of writing is not accessible for wheelchairs. The ruins of Greenhalgh Castle can be seen across the fields on the right. Return is by the same route. The bridge at the start of this section is a good vantage point to see the workings of the hydraulic river barrier, and the route as a whole gives excellent views across the open countryside towards the Forest of Bowland

### Points of Interest
Situated at the entrance to the car park the Garstang Discovery Centre has an exhibition on local countryside topics, a Tourist Information Centre and a Countryside Rangers Office. There are numerous leaflets and books available on the local area and the Discovery Centre is well worth a visit.

*The ruins of Greenhalgh Castle*

At 28 miles in length the River Wyre is reputedly the longest river in England whose estuary can be seen from its source. The river is particularly susceptible to flooding because it drains part of the Forest of Bowland where thin soils overlay impermeable rock. This means very little water can soak away into the ground so that after heavy rain the river receives more water than can be held within its banks. When there is a risk of flooding at the village of St Michael's-on-Wyre, downstream from Garstang, the hydraulic flood barrier is raised and the excess water is stored in the basin comprising the Rugby Field, Millennium Green and surrounding farm land. When the rains ease the flow of water in the river drops quickly and the water in the basin is released gradually so that the land in the basin can be returned to its normal uses.

Greenhalgh Castle was built in 1490 by Thomas Stanley, first Earl of Derby, to defend his estates in the area. During the English Civil War it was one of the last Royalist Castles in Lancashire to fall to Oliver Cromwell's forces, in 1645. It was then partly demolished to prevent it being used in the future and has remained in a ruined state to this day.

In 2001 Garstang became the first Fairtrade Town in the World, supporting exports from third world countries. The initiative was so successful that by 2006 over two hundred towns throughout the country had followed Garstang's example. Since then Fairtrade Towns have been established in Austria, Belgium, Canada, Finland, France, Ireland, Italy, Norway, Spain, Sweden, The Netherlands, and the United States. Garstang can be justifyably proud of its success in leading the World in this most important venture.

# 28. Glasson Dock, Lancaster

A bracing walk on an abandoned railway embankment along the shore of the Lune Estuary with wide-open views across the water towards Sunderland Point in the distance. There is also the option of taking the Lune millennium cycle track in the other direction from the car park, through Lancaster and along the bank of the river Lune up to Bull Beck car park, a distance of over 10 miles (see black dotted path on map opposite).

| | |
|---|---|
| **Distance** | 1½ miles to Glasson Dock there and back |
| **Path quality** | The car park and the ramp up to the picnic tables is tarmaced. The path from the car park to Glasson Dock is level and of fairly smooth compacted pebbles, and there is a fairly gentle slope down to the pavement at Glasson Dock |
| **Car Parking** | Travelling from Poulton-le-Fylde to Lancaster on the A588, turn left immediately in front of 'The Stork' inn, about 200 yards past the B5290 turn off to Glasson Dock. Corrick Lane, which passes in front of The Stork Inn leads directly into Condor Green Car Park in about ¼ mile |
| **Disabled toilet** | On the car park. RADAR key required |
| **Grid reference** | SD457562 |
| **Map** | OS Explorer Map 296 |

## Directions

The picnic tables on the Condor Green site are situated up a tarmac slope on the sea-wall embankment with long distance views down the river Lune towards Glasson Dock and the Lune Estuary beyond. In the

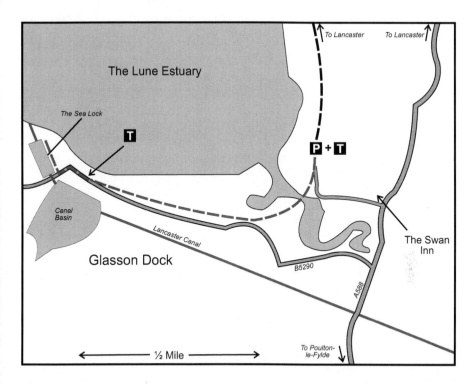

distance the distinctive twin buildings of Heysham Nuclear Power Station dwarf the opposite bank.

The path to Glasson Dock starts near the entrance to the car park, on the left hand side as you enter the car park. It follows the bed of an old railway line and almost immediately passes over a bridge over one of the estuary inlets. There are good estuary views all along here but the path is very exposed to the wind and an extra layer is advisable even in summer. When you reach the road it is just a short distance straight on to explore Glasson Dock itself. The dock surroundings are of level tarmac but care needs to be taken because of occasional traffic in this area.

## Points of Interest

Glasson Dock was built in 1787 because silting up of the river Lune prevented ships reaching the old port of Lancaster. In its heyday it was the largest port in North West England, and a link to the Lancaster canal was opened in 1826 to connect it to Lancashire's industrial heartland. It was also connected to Lancaster itself by a railway branch line in 1883. This ran until 1964, along the line that this particular walk now takes. In its early days imports included cotton, spices, tobacco and slaves. It is said that the furniture makers Waring and Gillow of Lancaster were successful commercially partly because of their use of cheap mahogany salvaged from the packing cases that some of these imports came in. The port is still in use today, bringing in animal foodstuffs and fertiliser and sending out coal to the Isle of Man and the Western Isles.

The Lune estuary itself is a Site of Special Scientific Interest, providing important habitats for a variety of migratory sea birds. The salt marshes around Condor Green are especially important because they are not grazed by sheep or cattle, resulting in a greater diversity of plants than is usually found along the Lancashire coastline.

*Glasson Dock*

# 29. Beacon Fell Country Park, Goosnargh

An area of rough hill top grazing and woods with views towards the Forrest of Bowland fells to the East and views across the Lancashire plain towards the coast to the West. The tracks on Beacon Fell are rough in places and are definitely not for the faint-hearted.

*The Visitor Centre*

### Directions

Go up the cobbled path towards the sculptured stone face opposite the car park and follow the yellow way-marked path to the concrete triangulation point at the summit of the fell. Return by the same route.

If you wish to attempt the circular route do it in the opposite direction so that you are going up the hazardous sections at point A and B,

| Distance | The circular wheelchair route to the summit is about ¾ of a mile. There are several miles of trails accessible by tramper scooters. See 'Points of Interest' below |
|---|---|
| Path quality | The tracks on Beacon Fell vary from good quality compacted earth and pebbles to rough stony tracks with some shallow steps and also some very muddy sections in wet weather. The route to the summit I have chosen for wheelchairs is steep and fairly rough in places including some cobbled sections, and the sections I have marked on the map as Point A and Point B should be avoided by all but the most adventurous. If at all possible, I would advise you to hire a tramper all-terrain mobility scooter. These are available free of charge |
| Car Parking | Follow the brown 'Beacon Fell' tourist signs from the village green at Inglewhite. When you get to Beacon Fell continue bearing right on the one-way system until you reach Fell House Car Park and the Bowland Visitor Centre. There are 2 disabled parking spaces |
| Disabled toilet | In the toilet block next to the Bowland Visitor Centre. A RADAR key is required |
| Grid reference | SD564426 |
| Map | OS Explorer Map OL41 |

which is easier than trying to come down them. You start by going up the shallow cobbled steps to the right of the car park (point A). I managed this in an ordinary powered wheelchair by using the grass to the right of the path. Turn left at the top of the hill and carry straight on to the summit. Point B consists of a steep roughly paved section

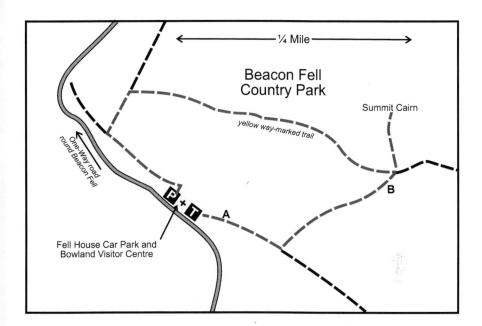

that I managed going up but that I wouldn't dream of going down, especially if it was wet. If you hire a tramper the warden will lend you a map showing the possible routes.

## Points of Interest

Beacon Fell is managed by Lancashire Countryside Service and, as mentioned above, it operates a scheme where disabled people can borrow a tramper all-terrain mobility scooter to access its country parks, free of charge.

The scheme operates at several locations throughout Lancashire and it is necessary to ring up a day or two beforehand to book a scooter, which is then available for up to two hours. Walks in this book where trampers are available include:

| | | |
|---|---|---|
| Walk 1 | Beacon Country Park | Tel: 01695 622794 |
| Walk 13 | Witton Country Park | Tel: 01254 55423 |
| Walk 20 | Wycoller Country Park | Tel: 01995 640577 |
| Walk 27 | Wyre Estuary Country Park | Tel: 01253 887220 |
| Walk 29 | Beacon Fell Country Park | Tel: 01995 640557 |

*A tramper at the summit of Beacon Fell*

The first time you borrow a tramper you are given an induction session lasting perhaps 20 minutes. You will require two passport-sized photographs which will be used for a membership card enabling you to use trampers at any of the locations.

# Walk 30. Dunsop Bridge

A fairly easy route into spectacular scenery at the heart of the Forest of Bowland. As you look around at the extensively wooded valley sides it's hard to believe you're still in Lancashire and not some remote Scottish Glen.

| | |
|---|---|
| **Distance** | 5 miles there and back |
| **Path quality** | Mostly level tarmac. The path through the trees leading to the footbridge over the river has a short rough section with prominent tree roots, but this can be avoided if the grass at the side is not too wet. The cattle grid just past the footbridge has a rough grassy track to the side gate which I found difficult to open unaided from my wheelchair |
| **Car Parking** | Travelling towards the Trough of Bowland from the south, turn right into Dunsop Bridge about 2¼ miles past Whitewell. Go over the bridge and the car park is about 150 yards along here on the left |
| **Disabled toilet** | On the car park. A RADAR key is required |
| **Grid reference** | SD661502 |
| **Map** | OS Explorer Map OL41 |

## Directions

From the car park turn right along the road back towards the bridge and, just before it, take a track to the right signposted 'Public Bridleway'. Follow this track across farmland to pass some buildings on your right and carry straight on, taking a path through a small wood by the side of a river. The path leads to a footbridge over the river and joins a tarmac farm access road. Turn right and follow this

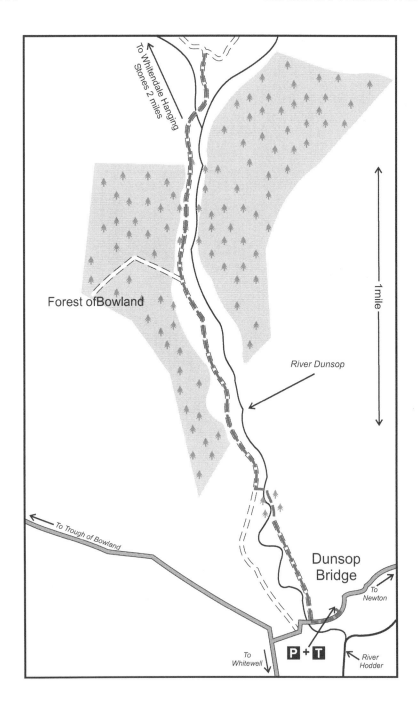

road up the valley for about 1¾ miles. At the first fork in the road bear right, but at the second fork it is advisable to return by the same route, as the tracks become steep beyond here. At this second fork in the track you are within two miles of the centre of Great Britain, at Whitendale Hanging Stones to the North of here.

## Points of Interest
Beside having been visited twice by the Queen this tiny village's main claim to fame is its nearness to the exact centre of Great Britain. To celebrate this fact British Telecom installed its 100,000th telephone box on the village green at Dunsop Bridge. A plaque reads 'You are calling from the BT payphone that marks the centre of Great Britain'.

*The path through farmland near the start of the walk*

# Walk 31. Trough of Bowland

A fine tarmac roadway leading to a wild and desolate upper valley in an area of outstanding natural beauty. It gives an impression of what the Trough of Bowland road must have looked like in the seventeenth century, when the Pendle Witches were brought along here to be imprisoned and subsequently hanged at Lancaster Castle (see 'Points of Interest' Walk 18)

| | |
|---|---|
| **Distance** | 1½ miles there and back |
| **Path quality** | The path as far as the water treatment plant is level tarmac. It then rises quite steeply to the upper valley and then levels out and deteriorates to a rough stony track |
| **Car Parking** | From Dunsop Bridge go over the bridge and up the hill. At the road junction turn right signposted 'Lancaster 15 Trough of Bowland'. After about 2 miles park in the large layby on the left by some trees at the bottom of the hill |
| **Disabled toilet** | At Dunsop Bridge 2 miles away. See Walk 30 |
| **Grid reference** | SD632512 |
| **Map** | OS Explorer Map OL41 |

## Directions

From the lay-by take the access road through the trees signposted 'Langden' and continue on up the hill past the water treatment plant. Carry straight on beyond the gate on a rough track which leads down to Langden Beck and then continues up the valley. Shortly after a

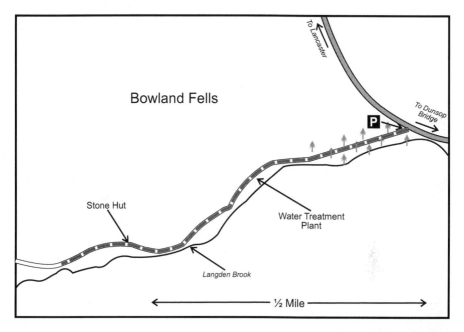

Bowland Fells

Stone Hut

Water Treatment
Plant

*Langden Brook*

To Lancaster

P

To Dunsop
Bridge

½ Mile

*The upper valley*

stone hut on the right, and then a second gate, the track rises steeply and a combination of poor surface and steep gradient makes further progress impracticable in a wheelchair. Return is by the same route. In my opinion even if the track is too rough for you it's worth doing the walk to just beyond the tarmac so that you can get an impression of the wild upper valley.

*The track through the trees*

# 32. Heysham

This walk starts down an old road to the sea, lined with seventeenth century cottages and an interesting and picturesque Church. The walk continues along the shoreline fringed with grassland towards Morecambe, which can be seen in the distance.

| | |
|---|---|
| **Distance** | 3 miles return from Heysham to the car park at the start of Walk 33 |
| **Path quality** | Tarmac all the way. There is a fairly steep path near the start of the coastal section, otherwise gradients are fairly gentle |
| **Car Parking** | Travelling from Morecambe to Heysham on the A589, turn right down Longlands Lane about ½ a mile past the junction with the B5273 to Lancaster. There is a brown tourist sign pointing down Longlands Lane which says 'Shore, St Peter's Church, St Patrick's Chapel, Heritage Centre'. Go down Longlands Lane and the car park is on the left at the bottom of the hill opposite the 'Curiosity Corner Tea Rooms'. There are 2 disabled spaces |
| **Disabled toilet** | At the entrance to the car park. A RADAR key is required |
| **Grid reference** | SD411614 |
| **Map** | OS Explorer Map 296 |

## Directions

Go down Main Street opposite the car park and continue down the hill past St Peter's Church, to swing round to the right into Bailey Lane. About 20 yards further on, turn left on a footpath signposted 'Whinnysty Lane ½'. This leads to the shore and the path then goes

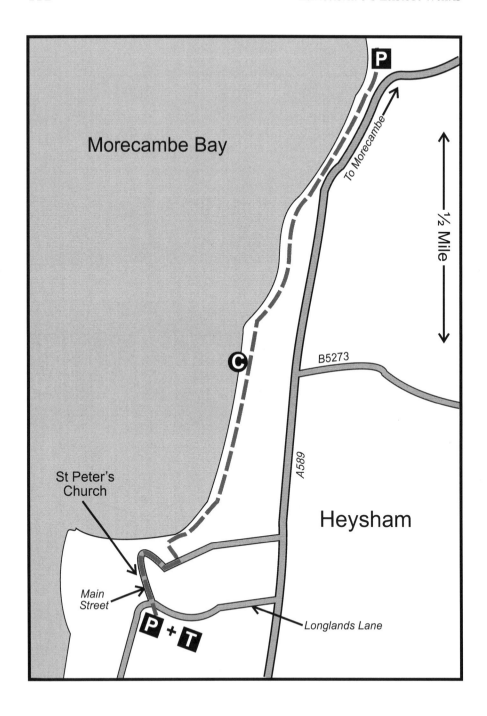

fairly steeply uphill to the top of a low cliff. Here you have the option of continuing along the path or of using the cycle track, which runs parallel to it and is somewhat smoother. The path continues along the shore, past a children's playground and on to join the car park at the start of Walk 33. Return is by the same route.

## Points of Interest

Main Street is the oldest part of Heysham, as dates on some of the cottages will testify. St Peter's Church is an absolute gem. It is built so close to the sea that there is a constant battle to strengthen the sea defences to stop some of the graves in the lower Churchyard being washed away. The Church has a wonderful view on a clear day from one of its side windows, which looks out across Morecambe Bay to the Lake District Hills in the distance. This view from Heysham Head is the subject of one of JMW Turner's paintings *Heysham and the Cumberland Mountains*. Turner visited Heysham in 1797 on a coach from Ulverston across the sands of Morecambe Bay – a journey that would be unthinkable today.

*Looking towards Morecambe from the top of the cliff*

There are graves in the Churchyard dating to Viking times and on the headland next to the Church, are a number of open graves hewn from solid rock, which are thought to date from the 11th century. Unfortunately, these are not accessible to wheelchair users. They are situated up a short cobbled lane that leads from the Church gate. The ruins of St Partick's Chapel and the stone graves near it are over the wall on the right, accessed by a flight of about nine or ten rough stone steps.

# 33. Morecambe Promenade

Despite Morecambe receiving something of a bad press in recent years, its refurbished promenade and the impressive long distance views of the Lake District hills, across Morecambe Bay, make this a delightful walk on a clear day.

| | |
|---|---|
| Distance | 6 miles return from the car park to Scalestones point, where the road turns away from the coast |
| Path quality | The promenade is level and paved/ tarmaced all the way |
| Car Parking | At the end of Morecambe promenade travelling towards Heysham, turn right in front of 'The Battery' public house and go straight on into the car park. There are 4 disabled parking spaces |
| Disabled toilet | The nearest one is about ¼ mile from the car park, back along the promenade. A RADAR key is required. The toilet is situated at the side of the toilet block facing the road and at the time of writing there is no signage on the door. There are further toilets along the promenade as shown on the map below |
| Grid reference | SD421636 |
| Map | OS Explorer Map 296 |

## Directions

From the car park go back towards the promenade and turn left. It is possible to continue along the promenade for up to 3 miles in each direction if you wish but the main points of interest, the Midland Hotel, the Eric Morecambe statue, and the RLNI lifeboat station are all within the first mile or so. If you do decide to go further, Happy Mount

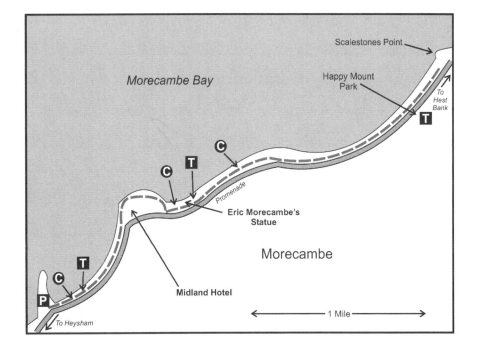

Park has a disabled toilet, a tearoom, and plenty of activities for children.

## Points of Interest

Morecambe had a long history as a thriving seaside resort, but suffered something of a decline in the last quarter of the twentieth century. It lost many of its attractions during this period. Its central pier was destroyed by fire, its other pier was destroyed by a storm, its much publicised 'Mr Blobby' attraction at Happy Mount Park survived for only three months, and its pleasure beach also had to close down. In 2003 it was voted the third worse town in the country to live in, after Kingston upon Hull and Cumbernauld. Since then, however, Morecambe has attracted sufficient investment to start to reinvent itself as a modern successful seaside town.

The iconic art deco Midland Hotel, which was built in 1933, has recently re-opened after a £7million restoration project. It incorporates a new outdoor swimming pool and has featured in the TV series 'Poirot' based on the Agatha Christie novels.

Refurbishment of the rest of the promenade includes a statue to one of its most famous sons, Eric Morecambe, who was so keen to promote his home town that he chose his stage name to reflect this.

The area of Morecambe Bay just north-east of the end of this walk, at Scalestones Point, is the location of the 2004 disaster when over twenty Chinese cockle pickers were drowned by the incoming tide. This is despite the fact that the lifeboat station at Morecambe had just over twelve months previously taken possession of the first hovercraft rescue vehicle in the country.

*Eric Morecambe's statue*

# 34. Williamson Park, Lancaster

An elegant Victorian Municipal Park on a hillside with spectacular views over the historic city of Lancaster and the River Lune. The Ashton Memorial, built by Lord Ashton in 1909 in memory of his late wife, provides a focal point at the top of the hill, and the nearby butterfly house provides a convenient refuge if it comes on to rain.

## Directions

From the car park take a path which leads back parallel with the road to the entrance gates, which you have just passed in the car. Turn right down the drive to go past an ornamental lake and on to the base

*The Ashton Memorial*

| | |
|---|---|
| **Distance** | There are several choices of path in this 54-acre park and, although there are a few steps, most of the paths are accessible for wheelchairs |
| **Path quality** | Some steep hills but most paths are tarmaced |
| **Car Parking** | From the M6 Junction 34 take signs for Lancaster and then at the one-way system take signs for the city centre, keeping in the left hand lane. Follow the road round to the left and, as it starts to go uphill, turn left up Moor lane (Brown signpost 'Pendle Witches Trail and Dukes Playhouse'). Continue uphill towards the monument on the skyline, go straight across the cross-roads up Wyresdale Road and continue on past the entrance gates to Williamson Park (Note: a left turn here leads to the Quernmore Road entrance – see 'Directions' below). The car park is a little way further on, on the left, signposted 'Ashton Memorial'. There are 7 disabled parking spaces. For an alternative disabled car park, close to the Ashton Memorial house and butterfly house, see 'Directions' below |
| **Disabled toilet** | On the car park. A RADAR key is required. A second disabled toilet is available inside the park in a toilet block at the side of the Ashton Memorial |
| **Grid reference** | SD488610 |
| **Map** | OS Explorer Map 296 |

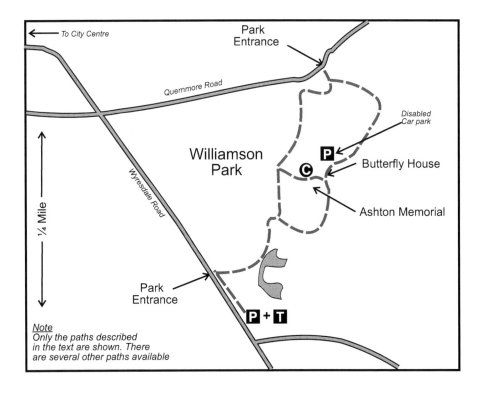

of the spectacular Ashton Memorial. The paths have been fairly level so far, but just past here the view opens up over Lancaster and you are now faced with the choice of steep uphill or steep downhill. If you choose uphill, it's a short, steep climb to the rear of the memorial and the butterfly house and café. If you choose downhill, and bear to the right, you eventually come to the Quernmore Road entrance to the park, and turning right here brings you back up to the butterfly house.

If you wish to see the butterfly house without the need to climb steep slopes, it is possible to enter the park by car, using the Quernmore Road entrance, and to park in a disabled car park at the top of the drive near the rear of the butterfly house. If you choose this option you will get a better impression of the park from the car and you will be able to see the views over Lancaster, but the level paths available from here are very limited.

## Points of Interest

Williamson Park was created on the site of an old Quarry, from which much of the stone was used in the building of Lancaster itself. The Park was created by the millionaire industrialist, James Williamson, at the end of the nineteenth century. He later took the title Lord Ashton and built the Ashton Memorial in memory of his wife Jessy. Its distinctive shape stands out on the skyline for miles around and it is known locally as the 'jelly mould' or 'the Taj Mahal of the North'. The butterfly house is located in the old Edwardian palm house and traces the life cycle of its many species of butterflies in a warm tropical forest setting.

# 35 Crook o' Lune Picnic Site, Caton

A delightful walk along the flat valley bottom of the river Lune with views up the valley towards the distinctive outline of Ingleborough Hill. Crook o' Lune itself is a dramatic horseshoe meander of the river. The subject of one of JMW Turner's famous paintings in the early nineteenth century, it is one of the most picturesque spots in the whole of Lancashire

## Directions
The path leaves the car park from opposite the toilet block, past a couple of picnic tables, with superb views over the river, and winds down to the cycle track below that follows the track of an old railway. Turn left and follow the cycle track, bypassing the village of Caton, and on for a mile or so until the cycle track ends at a ramp, to the

*The River Lune from the car park*

| | |
|---|---|
| **Distance** | 2½ miles there and back. The circular path is about ½ mile in total |
| **Path quality** | Level tarmac all the way. There is a fairly long slope down to the path from Crook O' Lune picnic site and a moderate slope up to the main road at Bull Beck picnic site. Note that this road has to be crossed to reach Bull Beck.<br>The circular walk is of crushed stone with gentle gradients. The actual path through the field is rather narrow in places.<br>The path down to the meadow at the water's edge is tarmac, but it has a couple of hairpin bends with adverse cambers which can be slippery in wet weather. The field itself is only really accessible for wheelchairs in dry weather |
| **Car Parking** | From the M6, Junction 34, take the A683 towards Kirkby Lonsdale and after about 2 miles turn left (Signpost: 'Crook o' Lune Picnic Site ¼' ). The car park is on the right, just over the bridge. There are 3 disabled parking spaces |
| **Disabled toilet** | On the far side of the toilet block. A RADAR key is required. There is also a disabled toilet (RADAR) at Bull Beck picnic site |
| **Grid reference** | SD521648 |
| **Map** | OS Explorer Map OL41 |

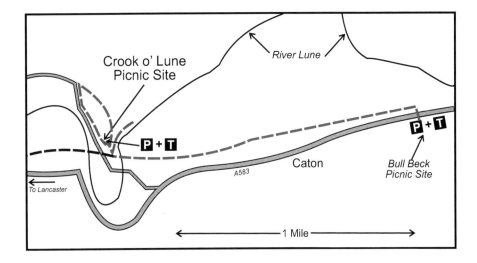

right, up to the main road. A couple of very minor lanes are crossed along the route, and the junctions are well marked to warn you to watch out for vehicles. As you reach the main A683, Bull Beck picnic site, with its snack bar and disabled toilets is directly across this busy road. Return is by the same route.

There is also a short circular walk from the car park. From the top of the access ramp, by the picnic tables, a gate on the left leads to a field path with lovely views over the river. The path curves round away from the river to meet a road. You can, however, take a path to the left behind a wall which runs along the side of a road and back to the car park.

The path down to the water's edge starts from the junction of the access ramp from the car park and the cycle track. It winds down to the water's edge and through a gate into the field beyond.

As with walk 28, there is the option, from Crook o' Lune picnic site, of taking this path (the Lune Millennium Cycle Track) in the opposite direction all the way through Lancaster to Glasson Dock, some 10 miles away (see black dotted path on map above).

# 36. Jenny Brown's Point, Silverdale

A pleasant walk down to the shore in Lancashire's most Northern Area of Outstanding Natural Beauty. The start of the walk, in extensive ancient woodland growing on limestone outcrops, is in stark contrast to the wide expanses of salt marsh at the other end of the walk.

## Directions

Retrace your steps back along the lane and up the hill to the bend near Wolf House Galleries, but keep straight on here down a minor lane (sighpost: 'Jenny Brown's Point'). Continue down this lane for about ¾ mile until, about 100 yards past a cattle grid, the road becomes private at a point where there is access down to the foreshore but, unfortunately, not for wheelchairs. Return is by the same route. As you return back up the lane away from the shore there are two or three kissing gates on the left, leading to an area of limestone grassland owned by the National Trust, called Jack Scout. There are also two or three kissing gates, on the left along this lane, leading into an area of limestone grassland owned by the National Trust, called Jack Scout. The second gate, opposite Ridgway Park School, is

*The limekiln on Jack Scout*

| Distance | 2 miles there and back |
|---|---|
| Path quality | Tarmac all the way with gentle to moderate slopes throughout. The optional detour onto Jack Scout is across rather bumpy but fairly level grassland which is probably too muddy in wet weather. The last time I visited here it was necessary to cross a veritable minefield of mole hills! |
| Car Parking | Travelling North from Lancaster on the A6, turn left at the traffic lights at Carnforth, down Market Street. After about 1¼ miles turn left in Warton ( signpost 'Arnside and Silverdale').. Continue for a couple of miles or so, over a level crossing and up to a T-junction where you turn left (road junction A) and shortly afterwards left again (Singpost Jenny Brown's Point). A further ½ mile brings you past the 'Wolf House Gallery' to a sharp right-hand bend down Lindeth Road. About 100 yards further on turn right down Woodwell Lane and carry straight on to the car park at the end of the lane |
| Disabled toilet | There is a disabled toilet for customers at the Wolf House Gallery and Tearooms but the nearest public disabled toilet is at Carnforth, on Market Street about 100 yards down from the A6 traffic lights, on the right hand side. A RADAR key is required |
| Grid reference | SD464744 |
| Map | OS Explorer Map OL7 |

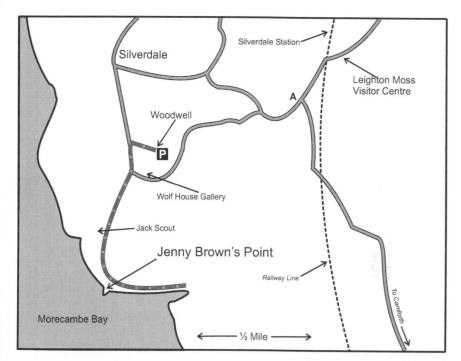

accessible for wheelchairs and, if you turn right to go parallel to the lane back up the hill, you come to an interesting and well-preserved limekiln, typical of the area.

There is a very descriptive information board detailing the history of the limekiln, and further ones at the entrance to Jack Scout about the natural history of the area.

## Points of Interest

About a mile from Woodwell, The Royal Society for the Protection of Birds has a site at Leighton Moss, which is well worth a visit. It has the largest reed-bed in north-west England, and this is home to some rare species of birds such as bitterns, bearded tits, and marsh harriers. There are good quality paths through the reeds leading to wheelchair accessible hides looking over the shallow lakes. The Visitor Centre has disabled parking spaces in front of it, and there is also a disabled toilet. Silverdale railway station is only about 100 yards away and the RSPB give free entry to visitors who come by public transport!

# More books from Simga Press:

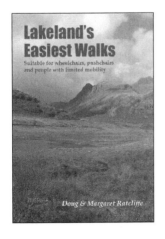

## Lakeland Easiest Walks

Suitable for wheelchairs, pushchairs and people with limited mobility

*Doug & Margaret Ratcliffe*

The Lake District and surrounding area has become far more accessible for wheelchairs and pushchairs in recent years. Although essentially a book for wheelchair users, these 38 specially selected short walks are all equally suitable for people with limited mobility and for very young children.

**£7.99**

## Easy Miles, No Steps No Stiles

In & around the Lake District

*Harriet Sharkey & John Barwise*

Easy Miles features 30 walks ideal for pushchairs, wheel- chairs and anyone who just wants an easy stroll. Each route has clear numbered maps, helpful information and photos.

**£7.99**

All of our books are all available on-line at **www.sigmapress.co.uk** or through booksellers. For a free catalogue, please contact:

**Sigma Leisure, Stobart House, Pontyclerc, Penybanc Road, Ammanford, Carmarthenshire SA18 3HP**
**Tel: 01269 593100   Fax: 01269 596116**

**info@sigmapress.co.uk        www.sigmapress.co.uk**